To Confess the Faith Today

To Confess the Faith Today

JACK L. STOTTS
and
JANE DEMPSEY DOUGLASS
editors

Westminster/John Knox Press
Louisville, Kentucky

First edition

Published by Westminster/John Knox Press
Louisville, Kentucky

PRINTED IN THE UNITED STATES OF AMERICA

9 8 7 6 5 4 3 2 1

Library of Congress Cataloging-in-Publication Data

To confess the faith today / Jack L. Stotts and Jane Dempsey Douglass, editors. — 1st ed.

p. cm.

ISBN 0-644-25098-X

1. Presbyterian Church (U.S.A.). Brief statement of faith.
2. Presbyterian Church (U.S.A.)—Creeds. 3. Presbyterian Church—United States—Creeds. 4. Reformed Church—United States—Creeds.
I. Stotts, Jack L. II. Douglass, E. Jane Dempsey.
BX8969.5.C65 1990
238'.5137—dc20 89-49524
CIP

Contents

Introduction
Jack L. Stotts and Jane Dempsey Douglass 7

A Brief Statement of Faith:
Presbyterian Church (U.S.A.)

Preface 21

The Statement
Draft Version 25

Revised Version 29

Essays on
"A Brief Statement of Faith"

1. *A Brief History of the Creedal Task:*
The Role of Creeds in Reformed Churches
John H. Leith 35

2. *The Ecumenical Significance of the Brief Statement of Faith*
David Willis-Watkins 50

3. *Contemporary Confession and Biblical Authority*
William C. Placher 64

4. *The Contemporaneity of the Brief Statement of Faith*
George H. Kehm 82

5. *Confessions in the Life of the Contemporary Church*
James D. Brown 93

6. *Inclusive Language and the Brief Statement of Faith: Widening the Margins in Our Common Confession*
Clarice J. Martin 107

7. *God Overcomes Death with Life*
Antoinette Clark Wire 130

Contributors 141

To Confess the Faith Today

Introduction

Jack L. Stotts
Jane Dempsey Douglass

Few of us knew one another. Oh, some of the names were familiar, books, articles, preaching, and poems having elevated them into prominence. Some wore invisible name tags with titles of evangelical, liberal, or conservative; scholar, pastor, or layperson; fearsome or feisty. These were often inaccurate as descriptions, but they were reflective of perceptions.

Yet there we were, called together by Dr. J. Randolph Taylor, the Moderator of the 195th General Assembly (1983) of the Presbyterian Church (U.S.A.). In May 1984 Dr. Taylor had appointed these twenty persons—soon to be twenty-one—as the Special Committee to Prepare a Brief Statement of the Reformed Faith for possible inclusion in the *Book of Confessions* of the Presbyterian Church (U.S.A.). The appointment of such a committee was one of the mandates of *The Plan for Reunion*, which, when adopted at the 1983 Assembly, brought a body too long divided together again. As with many contemporary "Reformed" confessions, reuniting was the occasion for a new confession of faith.

As part of his opening remarks, Dr. Taylor underscored his own sense of the importance of this committee's work for the theological integrity of the "new" church. A contemporary statement of belief was required if we were genuinely to come together around a common confession of faith in Jesus Christ as Lord, he contended. And if reunion was occasion, it was also opportunity. Dr. Taylor was persuasive in urging that the process of the denomination's consideration of a proposed statement of faith could have positive consequences for the theological vitality of the church, no matter what the final outcome. For through the debate and discussion required for amending the *Book of Confessions*, the denomination would have to focus explicitly on its beliefs and how those convictions should be stated and lived out in the contemporary world. "And wouldn't it be splendid," Dr. Taylor concluded, "if the Special Committee could bring its recommendations to the Bicentennial General Assembly in 1989?"

Five years later, in Philadelphia, Pennsylvania, at the 201st (the Bicentennial) General Assembly (1989), the Special Committee proposed "A Brief Statement of Faith: The Presbyterian Church (U.S.A.)." That gathering voted overwhelmingly to advance the proposal, along with recommendations for amendment, to the next stage of the extended procedure required to amend the confessional standards. Another special committee (the Committee of 15) was appointed to study, review, and possibly revise the draft, in consultation with the existing Special Committee, and to report its recommendations to the subsequent General Assembly. What follows at the conclusion of this Introduction is the draft submitted to the 1989 Assembly, with a preface.

As is true with every extended document that comes before a General Assembly—or, for that matter, any ecclesiastical or civil governing body—the end product has a history of development that is not readily apparent. Behind the document as a whole and within each of its parts lie issues that claimed time, energy, research, argumentation, prayer, and, at times, compromise between competing interests or perspectives. Such issues are often soaked with passion as well as shaped by "sweet reasonableness." In fact, one would be wary of any Christian statement of faith that did not express and provoke contentions of the heart and the head. Probes into the core of who we are and what we believe will inevitably touch sensitive nerve endings.

So it is with "A Brief Statement of Faith." Its relatively sparse and yet evocative phrasing simultaneously reflects and invites exploration. There is rich theological ore to be mined in every sentence, in many phrases, in particular words, and even in punctuation marks! It is true that "A Brief Statement" can be read quickly. But it can also introduce and project the reader into extended theological discussion about what we Presbyterians believe and what we are to do. There is a theological and evangelical depth to the document that may not be readily apparent at first sight.

It was Justice Holmes of the United States Supreme Court who once commented, "For simplicity this side of complexity I would not give you a fig; but for simplicity beyond complexity, I would give you almost anything." And the simplicity of this Statement is one, we believe, that has gone through and beyond complexity to a simplicity of depth. The Statement is the harvest of complex theological reflection and inquiry, deposited in language that the committee hopes will be at once accessible to "ordinary" church members, expressive of the historic faith of the church, and orienting of the church toward the future. This introduction and the following essays unpack something of the context and content of this simple document.

The Brief Statement draft is the work of a committee that became a community. The Special Committee, meeting regularly over a five-year period, became a community that centered its common life around worship, theological inquiry, and ecclesiastical concern. Its boundaries were, furthermore, porous, as consultations and hearings gave opportunity for churches and ecumenical partners to respond to drafts. Written evaluations—over 15,000—poured onto the committee's table. Within that life together, the committee wrestled with multiple questions, some of which are surveyed below.

At the outset several significant decisions were made which set the pattern for later work. One was that of the structure for the contemporary statement of faith. The committee decided to use the apostolic benediction as the ordering principle, reflecting thereby its commitment to the trinitarian and biblical grounding of the Reformed confessional tradition. And by its phrasing of the opening line, "In life and in death we belong to God," the committee echoed the first question and answer in the Heidelberg Catechism, signaling the importance of a contemporary creed's continuity with earlier confessions. That line also affirms God's Lordship, giving a forward trajectory to the responsibility borne by Christians, individually and corporately in the church, to struggle against the powers of death.

Though the Statement often echoes earlier confessions, it introduces aspects of our common faith that were missing in earlier creeds or that seem to us today to need greater emphasis than they have previously received.

The first example is in the section dealing with the person of Christ. We have been accustomed with the Apostles' Creed to move from the incarnation of Christ directly to his suffering on the cross. Our generation, however, has become particularly conscious of the significance of Christ's earthly ministry as a sign of the reign of God in the midst of human life. Liberation theologies today emphasize Christ's bringing of good news to the poor and his life of loving service among the outcasts of society. Because Christ's teaching and his announcing of God's reign are so essential to the whole Reformed tradition of theology, lines 7 through 23 are needed to bring this aspect of Christ's work regularly to our consciousness as we confess our faith together.

A second part of the particularity of this Statement is represented by line 53. Here, perhaps for the first time in the history of the church, a confessional statement declares as a matter of the faith of the church that the Holy Spirit calls women as well as men to all the public ministries of the church. This declaration consciously repudiates older confessional teaching. For example, the Second Helvetic Confession explicitly disallows women pastors: "We teach that baptism should not be administered in the Church by women or midwives. For Paul deprived women of ecclesiastical duties, and baptism has to do with these" (Chapter XX). The Scots Confession joins its voice in declaring that Roman Catholic priests are not true ministers because "they even allow women, whom the Holy Ghost will not permit to preach in the congregation, to baptize" (Chapter XXII). But "A Brief Statement of Faith" sturdily elevates to confessional status a recognition of God's gifts for ministry to both women and men, thereby insisting on gender equality in the church.

Underlying such a departure from tradition is a clarification of Christian teaching on the creation, lines 26–29. Though the church has always taught that humanity is made in the image of God, over the centuries theologians have often claimed that some sorts of persons possess the image of God more fully than others. Clarity that all human beings are equally made in the image of God, regardless of sex, race, or innate abilities, is necessary to confront and reject claims that continue to be made in our world today for women's inherent inferiority to men, or for the natural superiority of one race over another, or for the less than human status of the

disabled. God's intention for humanity to live in community can be realized only when each person learns to recognize the image of God in every other person and respect it.

Another old but recurring issue provoked strong debate within the committee: "How does one speak of God?" The sense of awe before God and the recognition that humans are not God, and that God's ways are not our ways, led the people of Israel never to speak the name of God. Holiness eluded naming, even though speaking of God was essential. And Christians—in different ways—have joined their Hebrew forebears and friends in remembering the injunction not to make images of God, whose being is beyond human capacity to depict in word or figure. Indeed, the fear that humans would collapse the reality of God into a human designation or nomenclature has given all our speaking of God a proper theological tentativeness. Nevertheless, in both our piety and our theology we naturally become attached to powerful and familiar ways of speaking of God. Then when we are getting too comfortable, a new way of speaking arouses our minds and challenges our views of God and of ourselves.

Such a challenge is posed today by the search for a way of speaking about God that is not, even unintentionally, gender exclusive. Such exclusiveness would be a form of idolatry. In the section on the first person of the Trinity, lines 24 through 42, the committee struggled to find gender-inclusive God-language on which all could agree. No member contended for anything other than gender-inclusive terms with reference to humankind, which have long been a matter of policy in the Presbyterian Church (U.S.A.). But the question of God-language is different. There the denomination and its governing bodies have no settled opinion; the policy guidelines are less clear and less generally accepted. Rather, the search continues with vigor, accompanied often by pain, for appropriate ways to speak about and to address God. So it was in the committee. As a microcosm of the church theologically, the committee recognized that it could not propose a resolution to this issue. To do so would be premature. But what was called for was a way or ways to signal the question as significant theologically and, with reference to issues of justice, consequential. To preserve the dissonance about this matter was to affirm the discussion as legitimate.

Therefore, the language about God chosen by the committee was designed to encourage a positive context for debate. A constructive model of expanding language about God, to include female as well as male images for God, became a part of the proposal. God is "like a mother who cannot forget her nursing child, like a father who runs to welcome the prodigal home." These images for speaking about God were drawn from the variety of images within scripture itself. In the final doxology (line 68), ancient trinitarian liturgical language of the church universal—with its male imagery—is recognized as continuing to play a role in connecting our worship to the long stream of Christian history. But the note on line 69 acknowledges that already this language has become "foreign" in many of our congregations.

In adopting the approach described above, the committee had no illusions that it had the last word to offer on this substantial topic. It did acknowledge that any confession of faith developed in the latter years of the twentieth century would be sorely deficient if it failed to encourage and help the church to wrestle with the issue.

Another distinctive aspect of "A Brief Statement" is the nature of its attention to creation. In earlier creeds there has often been a quick jump from creation to fall. But in lines 24 through 42, the affirmation that God created the world good is joined with God's intention for all people to live as one

community, relating to each other in equality and mutuality, as we have seen. There follows the confession of human distortion of the good creation, even to the extremity of threatening death to the life of the planet as we know it. "We deserve God's judgment" (line 35) is an existential and ontological declaration of our condition before the Creator. Yet God who is merciful and just has the last as well as the first word. That word is the working of God to restore the creation to its original condition, returning humans to their proper destiny of life together. This activity of God is provident for humans and for the entire created order.

There is in this section on creation also a theme that has only very recently found its place in Reformed confessions, the stewardship of creation; though it is here put negatively, it has in the context of God's restoring work a positive thrust. To admit that (line 34) we threaten death to the planet entrusted to our care is to reaffirm our God-given responsibility for this wounded planet. No theme of human responsibility is more important than this in an era of environmental degradation and nuclear threat. It is this theme of stewardship that is picked up and developed by several of the essays that follow, testifying to its importance for the whole committee.

The section on God the Holy Spirit (lines 43–64) compresses into twenty-two brief lines a wealth of convictions Presbyterians hold. There is reference to the free and surprising work of the Spirit, "everywhere the giver and renewer of life." The Spirit's gifts are not in this statement confined to the church. There is the doctrine of Christian freedom, a freedom that delivers human beings from every sort of bondage and unites us in the one church of Jesus Christ. The theme linking Christian freedom and Christian responsibility with a doctrine of the one church affirms the ecumenical stance that is essential, not elective, for Presbyterians.

The structure of the section on the life of the church as a worshiping community (lines 48–53) emphasizes the Reformed sense that the continuing lively working of the Spirit is essential to every aspect of its ongoing life. Not only did the Holy Spirit long ago inspire the biblical authors, but the Spirit also confirms in us today that the Word of God can be heard in the scriptures. Only with the Spirit's enlivening of our faith can we receive through the scriptures God's word to us; and only so can water and bread and wine become the means of grace to us, "visible words" by which we truly receive the life renewal promised by Christ. Indeed, in the "living water" and the "bread of life" we see that the Holy Spirit makes Christ himself present to us.

Unlike the ancient creeds but in the tradition of the sixteenth-century Reformed confessions, the Statement moves on to speak of the mission of the church. Christians gathered as church and dispersed in the world in their daily work are called and empowered by the Holy Spirit to engage in witness to Christ's Lordship: announcing the gospel and participating in God's work of transformation and renewal of all of human society until God's intention for the world will be visible to all. Like Reformed people over the centuries, we declare that Christian life, however costly, is an act of gratitude made possible by the life of the Spirit in us.

Running through the entire Statement is a theme common to several contemporary Reformed confessions. That theme is life and death: life given and renewed by God, death overcome and defeated by God. It is no coincidence that our belonging to God in life and death should be so critical to Reformed people today in a world frightened by impending death and desperately hoping for life.

There are theological and devotional riches to mine in "A Brief Statement of Faith," but this Statement also invites those who confess to bring their own gifts of faith, knowledge, and reflection to bear on its content. To do so is to engage in theological reflection and discussion that can and will deepen piety and enlarge understanding of what "I" and "we" believe as Presbyterians.

The essays that follow were designed to get behind the compact Statement of Faith to its more luxuriant background, to expose something of the learned and yeasty thinking that found its way into the words, phrasing, and organization of the document. Each author was a member of the Special Committee and reflects the discussions internal to its life. Each one, however, speaks only for herself or himself. Each explores a question or an issue that will help the reader to understand both the context and the content of the Statement. Each of the essays can be read on its own, but taken together they furnish the serious student of the Statement with tools that will help to interpret the document's place in the Reformed heritage; to explore issues of complexity with which the committee struggled before arriving at the simplicity of the wording; and to be stimulated to "think forward" from the words to their meaning for faithful witness to Jesus Christ as Lord.

Finally, the following essays clearly arise from a Presbyterian Church (U.S.A.) experience. The issues they address, however, have no exclusive denominational boundaries. Questions such as gender-inclusive God-language, the interpretation of scripture, the image of God, and the contemporary context for confessing the Christian faith are genuinely ecumenical, common concerns no matter what one's particular faith community. Equally pertinent in this regard is the Special Committee's acknowledgment from the beginning of its work that any statement of faith authentically "Reformed" would be genuinely ecumenical, confessing the faith of the one church of Jesus Christ. There is every reason to hope, therefore, and good reason to believe, that these essays are indeed resources for studying both "A Brief Statement of Faith: Presbyterian Church (U.S.A.)" and also issues relative to confessing the faith regardless of the denominational setting. To confess the faith today is a responsibility for all the people of God.

A Brief Statement of Faith: Presbyterian Church (U.S.A.)

Preface

In 1983 the two largest Presbyterian churches in the United States reunited. *The Plan for Reunion* called for the preparation of a brief statement of the Reformed faith for possible inclusion in the *Book of Confessions*. This statement is therefore not intended to stand alone, apart from the other confessions of our church. It does not pretend to be a complete list of all our beliefs, nor does it explain any of them in detail. It is designed to be confessed by the whole congregation in the setting of public worship, and it may also serve pastors and teachers as an aid to Christian instruction. It celebrates our rediscovery that, for all our undoubted diversity, we are bound together by a common faith and a common task.

The faith we confess unites us with the one, universal church. The most important beliefs of Presbyterians are

---

The preface and the appendix [which is not reproduced here] do not have confessional authority. The appendix provides cross-references which will enable the reader to place the affirmations of "A Brief Statement of Faith" in the context of the Reformed tradition.

those we share with other Christians, and especially with other evangelical Christians who look to the Protestant Reformation as a renewal of the gospel of Jesus Christ. Diversity remains. But we are thankful that in our time the many churches are learning to accept, and even to affirm, diversity without divisiveness, since the whole counsel of God is more than the wisdom of any individual or any one tradition. The Spirit of Truth gives new light to the churches when they are willing to become pupils together of the Word of God. This statement therefore intends to confess the catholic faith.

We are convinced that to the Reformed churches a distinctive vision of the catholic faith has been entrusted for the good of the whole church. Accordingly, "A Brief Statement of Faith" includes the major themes of the Reformed tradition (such as those mentioned in the *Book of Order*, "Form of Government," Chapter 2) without claiming them as our private possession, just as we ourselves hope to learn and to share the wisdom and insight given to traditions other than our own. And as a confession that seeks to be both catholic and Reformed, the statement (following the apostle's blessing in 2 Cor. 13:14) is a trinitarian confession in which the grace of Jesus Christ has first place as the foundation of our knowledge of God's sovereign love and our life together in the Holy Spirit.

No confession of faith looks merely to the past; every confession seeks to cast the light of a priceless heritage on the needs of the present moment, and so to shape the future. Reformed confessions, in particular, when necessary even reform the tradition itself in the light of the Word of God. From the first, the Reformed churches have insisted that the renewal of the church must become visible in the transformation of human lives and societies. Hence "A Brief Statement of Faith" lifts up concerns that call most urgently for the church's attention in our time. The church is not a refuge from the world; an elect people is chosen for the blessing of the nations. A sound confession, therefore, proves itself as it nurtures commitment to the church's mission, and as the confessing church itself becomes the body by which Christ continues the blessing of his earthly ministry.

The Statement

(Draft Version)

In life and in death we belong to God.
Through the grace of our Lord Jesus Christ,
the love of God,
and the communion of the Holy Spirit,
we believe in the one triune God,
in whom alone we trust.

We trust in Jesus Christ,
fully God, fully human.
Jesus proclaimed the reign of God:
preaching good news to the poor
and teaching by word and deed,
healing the sick
and eating with outcasts,

At the time this book went to press, the Brief Statement had not yet reached its final form. The draft above is the form that was current during the summer and fall of 1989 and was the basis for the essays in this book. The revised version that follows was added in January 1990 but was still subject to change by the General Assembly later in 1990.

14 forgiving sinners
15 and calling all to repent and believe the gospel.
16 Unjustly condemned for blasphemy and sedition,
17 Jesus was crucified,
18 suffering the depths of human pain
19 and giving his life for the sins of the world.
20 God raised him from the dead,
21 vindicating his sinless life,
22 breaking the power of sin and evil,
23 delivering us from death to life eternal.

24 We trust in God,
25 whom Jesus called Abba, Father.
26 In sovereign love God created the world good
27 and makes everyone,
28 male and female, of every race and people,
29 equally in God's image to live as one community.
30 But we rebel against God:
31 refusing to love God and neighbor,
32 corrupting ourselves,
33 exploiting others,
34 and threatening death to the planet entrusted to our care.
35 We deserve God's judgment.
36 Yet God rules with justice and mercy to redeem creation.
37 Through Abraham and Sarah God chose a covenant people
38 to bless all the families of the earth.
39 As heirs in Christ of the covenant,
40 we know God remains faithful still,
41 like a mother who cannot forget her nursing child,
42 like a father who runs to welcome the prodigal home.

43 We trust in God the Holy Spirit,
44 everywhere the giver and renewer of life,
45 who sets us free to love God and neighbor
46 and binds us together with all believers
47 in the one body of Christ, the church.
48 The same Spirit
49 who inspired the prophets and apostles
50 rules our faith and life in Christ through Scripture,
51 baptizes us in living water,
52 feeds us with the bread of life,
53 and calls women and men to all ministries of the church.
54 In a broken and fearful world
55 the Spirit gives us courage
56 to witness to Christ as Lord and Savior,
57 to unmask idolatries in church and culture,
58 to work for justice, freedom, and peace,
59 and to claim all of life for Christ.
60 In gratitude to God
61 we strive to serve Christ in our daily tasks
62 and to live holy and joyful lives,
63 even as we watch for God's new heaven and new earth,
64 praying, "Come, Lord Jesus!"

65 With believers in every time and place,
66 we rejoice that nothing in life or in death
67 can separate us from the love of God in Christ Jesus our Lord.
68 Glory be to the Father, and to the Son, and to the Holy Spirit. Amen.*

---

(69) *Instead of saying this line, congregations may wish to sing a version of the Gloria.

The Statement

(Revised Version)

1 In life and in death we belong to God.
2 Through the grace of our Lord Jesus Christ,
3 the love of God,
4 and the communion of the Holy Spirit,
5 we trust in the one triune God, the Holy One of Israel,
6 whom alone we worship and serve.

7 We trust in Jesus Christ,
8 fully human, fully God.
9 Jesus proclaimed the reign of God:
10 preaching good news to the poor
11 and release to the captives,
12 teaching by word and deed
13 and blessing the children,

The statement above was unanimously adopted on January 12, 1990, by the Special Committee to Prepare a Brief Statement of the Reformed Faith (appointed 1984) and the Committee of 15 (appointed 1989) for submission to the 202nd General Assembly (1990).

14 healing the sick
15 and binding up the brokenhearted,
16 eating with outcasts,
17 forgiving sinners,
18 and calling all to repent and believe the gospel.
19 Unjustly condemned for blasphemy and sedition,
20 Jesus was crucified,
21 suffering the depths of human pain
22 and giving his life for the sins of the world.
23 God raised this Jesus from the dead,
24 vindicating his sinless life,
25 breaking the power of sin and evil,
26 delivering us from death to life eternal.

27 We trust in God,
28 whom Jesus called Abba, Father.
29 In sovereign love God created the world good
30 and makes everyone equally in God's image,
31 male and female, of every race and people,
32 to live as one community.
33 But we rebel against God; we hide from our Creator.
34 Ignoring God's commandments,
35 we violate the image of God in others and ourselves,
36 accept lies as truth,
37 exploit neighbor and nature,
38 and threaten death to the planet entrusted to our
care.
39 We deserve God's condemnation.
40 Yet God acts with justice and mercy to redeem
creation.
41 In everlasting love,
42 the God of Abraham and Sarah chose a covenant
people
43 to bless all families of the earth.
44 Hearing their cry,

45 God delivered the children of Israel
46 from the house of bondage.
47 Loving us still,
48 God makes us heirs with Christ of the covenant.
49 Like a mother who will not forsake her nursing child,
50 like a father who runs to welcome the prodigal home,
51 God is faithful still.

52 We trust in God the Holy Spirit,
53 everywhere the giver and renewer of life.
54 The Spirit justifies us by grace through faith,
55 sets us free to accept ourselves and to love God and neighbor,
56 and binds us together with all believers
57 in the one body of Christ, the church.
58 The same Spirit
59 who inspired the prophets and apostles
60 rules our faith and life in Christ through Scripture,
61 engages us through the Word proclaimed,
62 claims us in the waters of baptism,
63 feeds us with the bread of life and the cup of salvation,
64 and calls women and men to all ministries of the church.
65 In a broken and fearful world
66 the Spirit gives us courage
67 to pray without ceasing,
68 to witness among all peoples to Christ as Lord and Savior,
69 to unmask idolatries in church and culture,
70 to hear the voices of peoples long silenced,
71 and to work with others for justice, freedom, and peace.

72 In gratitude to God, empowered by the Spirit,
73 we strive to serve Christ in our daily tasks
74 and to live holy and joyful lives,
75 even as we watch for God's new heaven and new earth,
76 praying, "Come, Lord Jesus!"

77 With believers in every time and place,
78 we rejoice that nothing in life or in death
79 can separate us from the love of God in Christ Jesus our Lord.

80 Glory be to the Father, and to the Son, and to the Holy Spirit. Amen.*

---

(81) *Instead of saying this line, congregations may wish to sing a version of the Gloria.

Essays on "A Brief Statement of Faith"

A Brief History of the Creedal Task: The Role of Creeds in Reformed Churches

1

John H. Leith

Christianity has always been a "creedal" religion in that it has always been theological.[1] It was rooted in the theological tradition of ancient Israel, which was unified by historical credos and declaratory affirmations of faith. A brief excursion into three periods of the church's confessional life will illustrate certain features of creeds that are important for the church today.

Early Creeds

Christian confession began among the disciples of Jesus as they gave expression to their developing realization that Jesus was unique among men and women, and of unique importance for their relationship to God. "In putting their convictions into words, the disciples ascribed to Jesus the loftiest concept known to them, namely Christ."[2] This witness to what God has done in Jesus of Nazareth was from the beginning the decisive mark of Christians. It made them liable unto death; as the early Christians put it, they were persecuted for the "name." Origen, the third-century theologian for whom martyrdom was an ever-present possibility, declared, "It is better to honour God with lips when one's heart is far from God than to honour him with the heart and not to make confession with the mouth unto salvation."[3] The early Christians reserved martyrdom, not for those who died on behalf of a good cause, but for those who died for their witness to God's work in creation and redemption. To confess Jesus as Christ, for these early Christians, was at the heart of their lives.

Thus, creeds are first of all an expression of the life of the Christian community. "In confessing his faith through the medium of a creed, the believer is expressing his deepest self."[4] The confession of faith, as Karl Barth has written, is the praise of God, an acknowledgment of the reality of the one true and living God.[5] A confession of Christian faith is not a statement of how we feel, or of how we adjust to the world, or of what we propose to do. It is an acknowledgment of the gracious presence of God as our Creator, Judge, and Redeemer. It is our YES to the presence of God in Jesus Christ. It is therefore, first of all, an act of praise and worship.

The earliest Christian creeds were very simple statements pointing to the significance of Jesus Christ: Jesus is the Christ (Mark 8:29) or Jesus is Lord (1 Cor. 12:3). The New Testament is replete with such statements, reflecting the variety in the early churches' experience and communal settings. Yet more basic than the variety was the unity of the creedlike confessions, which gradually developed in a trinitarian pattern in the interrogatory forms of baptism and in the declaratory forms of the catechumen classes. Local congregations had their own creeds with idiosyncratic variations, but always affirming the trinitarian faith.[6] These congregational creeds became the basis for the two creeds of the early church that are best known to the church today. In the East, the Council of Nicaea in 325 took one such creed and inserted into it phrases that rejected Arianism—and that affirmed that Jesus Christ was truly God, "of the same substance as the Father." The Nicene Creed was the first creed with conciliar authority, and it became the most universal of all Christian creeds. In the West, the dominance of the church at Rome imposed the pattern of the early Roman creed on all the provincial churches. Our present Apostles' Creed is the Roman creed as it was modified in southwestern France some time in the seventh century.

The early creeds grew out of the life of the church. Their sources are often unknown. But as expressions of the church's faith, they served many essential functions in the church's life. One was for use in worship.

The worship of the church has been a primary occasion that called for the development of creeds. The confession of faith is an essential moment in the life of the Christian and of the church, for in the confession the believer speaks out in the presence of other believers and of the world, declaring the deepest commitments of the heart and mind. In confessions, believers take their stand individually and together, commit their lives, declare what they believe to be true, affirm their ultimate loyalty, and defy every false claim upon their lives. Thus, the confession of faith is a seal of faith and of the courage of faith. The liturgy is "the affirmation, acknowledgment, and approval, not of any god, but of Emmanuel, so that it takes the form of worthy and salutary confession; and therefore even more particularly as the element in which the community says expressly to itself and the world that the main concern in its whole existence, and therefore its assembling too, is with this affirmation and confession."[7]

Creeds have always been associated with the sacraments of baptism and the Lord's Supper. The creedal form that was apparently most commonly used in the baptismal rites of the second and third centuries was interrogatory. Baptism from the beginning took place in the context of the confession of the baptized and in the context of the community's confession of faith. From the fifth century on, the Nicene Creed was a part of the celebration of the sacrament of the Lord's Supper.

Another function of creeds was their usefulness in teaching. The teaching ministry had as its essential function the handing on of the creed. In the catechumen class, the high moment came when the creed was "traditioned" to those who were becoming Christians, and then the catechumens "rendered" back the creed as their own.[8] The catechetical use of the creed played an important part in the movement from the interrogatory creed of baptism to the declaratory creed of instruction. Alongside the declaratory creeds, which were precise and fixed in form and used in worship, the church also had rules of faith, which were more flexible in form and content and of greater length. They served as guides for preaching and for instruction.

Creeds have also served as a guide for the interpretation of scripture and for reflection upon the meaning of faith. The creeds distinguished what was centrally important in scripture from the peripheral, and they put the message of scripture together in a coherent fashion. The creeds are the record of the churches' interpretation of the scripture in the past and the authoritative guide to its interpretation in the present.

Creeds were also the Christian community's attempt to deal with heresy: that is, the distortion, the dilution, the truncation, and the outright denial of Christian faith. Heresy is so important a factor in the origin of creeds that it has tempted many commentators to exaggerate its role.[9] As was said long ago, creeds are signposts to heresies. A task of the creed was to defend the church against heresy. The creed had a negative role in shutting the heretic out and setting the boundaries within which authentic Christian theology and life can take place. Heresies, on the other hand, played a positive role in the development of creeds. They made the church think through theological issues when it did not want to do so, and required the church to exercise care in theological language.

Creeds are also a standard, a battle cry, a testimony, and a witness to the world. In the ancient church, they were the occasion for the Christian witness in the face of persecution, as in our time the Barmen Declaration was the testimony of confessing Christians against the Germanization of the faith under National Socialism. In this sense, the creed is a marching song. In this fact resides some of the truth in the assertion that creeds ought to be sung.

Creeds also serve the purpose of expressing identity. They proclaim the faith of the Christian to the world, and they also distinguish Christians from non-Christians. In reciting the creeds of the church, believers identify themselves not only with those in their immediate presence but with Christian believers everywhere and in all times, with the church triumphant as well as the church militant.

Creeds grow out of the life of the church, serving to express its faith, but creeds have also been used as a test of orthodoxy. In the Arian controversy in the fourth century, for example, the Nicene Creed became not simply the church's confession but the church's test to exclude beliefs that threatened the very existence of the church itself. Yet creeds as tests of orthodoxy are secondary to creeds as expressions of the church's faith. They can be tests of orthodoxy only insofar as they are authentically the expression of the faith of the community.

The most important creeds of the early church, all of which were reaffirmed in the Protestant Reformation, were the Apostles' Creed, the Nicene Creed, the Chalcedonian Definition, and the Athanasian Creed.

Reformed Creeds

The Protestant Reformers understood the human problem to be basically theological, and they sought to give theological answers to the problem. Efforts to explain the Reformation in terms of economics, politics, the conflicts of social classes, or the rise of the cities are all secondary to the theological character of the Reformation. This great renewal of the church was theological and therefore creedal from the beginning.

The first confessions of the Reformation took the form of theses, prepared to facilitate debate and to present clearly and precisely the affirmations of Protestants. The event that more than any other represented the beginning of the Reformation was Martin Luther's nailing the Ninety-five Theses to the church door at Wittenberg on October 31, 1517.[10] Theses affirming the faith also played a prominent role in the Reformation in Switzerland: Zwingli's Sixty-seven Articles of Religion (1523), the Ten Conclusions of Bern (1528), and the Lausanne Articles (1536). Confessions also took the form of letters addressed to rulers, such as Zwingli's confession to Charles V (1530) and the confession to Francis I (1531).

The Genevan Confession of 1537 prepared by Farel and John Calvin was designed as a public affirmation of faith that was to be made by all inhabitants of Geneva. Here the confession served a social as well as a religious purpose, binding together all the residents of the city.

In the Reformation, catechisms were important confessional statements. Luther's Small and Large Catechisms played a very important part in the public affirmation of faith, as well as in the handing on of the faith through teaching. Calvin likewise prepared at the very beginning of his ministry the Catechism of 1537 in declaratory form and wrote a question-and-answer catechism in 1542 for Christian instruction.

Comprehensive statements of faith began to appear as

Protestant communities matured. Chief among these confessions are: the Tetrapolitan Confession (1520), the Confession of Basel (1534), the First Helvetic Confession (1536), the Zurich Consensus (1549), the Gallican Confession (1554), the Scots Confession (1560), the Belgic Confession (1561), the Heidelberg Catechism (1563), and the Second Helvetic Confession (1566).

The Reformation confessions were not sectarian. They were intended to be catholic, to confess the one faith of the whole church. They all presupposed and appropriated in their structure the theological work and the creeds of the ancient catholic church. They could not have been written apart from the theological developments of the Middle Ages. No Protestant confession ever set out to give a Lutheran or Reformed or German or French statement of the faith. Yet each intended to state the one faith of the Christian community in its particular situation.

The Reformed confessions are distinguished by their great variety and their number. Reformed Christians generally rejected the notion of any universal Christian statement. They did not want to give final authority to any statement that they believed was limited by time and place as well as by human finiteness and sin. They were clear in their own minds that creeds were always subordinate to scripture and that no creed should have exaggerated pretensions.

Heinrich Bullinger (1504–1575) and Leo Judae (1482–1542) are said to have signed the First Helvetic Confession with this comment:

> We wish in no way to prescribe for all the church through these articles a single rule of faith. For we acknowledge no other rule of faith than Holy Scripture. We agree with whoever agrees with this although he uses different expressions from our confession. For we should have regard for the fact itself and for the truth, not for the words. We grant to everyone the freedom to use his own expression which is suitable

> for his church and will make use of this freedom ourselves, at the same time defending the true sense of this confession against distortions.[11]

Theologians have despaired of writing *the* theology of Reformed confessions; only theologies of Reformed confessions can be written. Furthermore, no one can provide an official list of Reformed confessions, as no one has the authority to set boundaries. The Reformed community produced at least fifty confessions of some note in the first fifty years.

These Reformed confessions differ greatly also in style. Some are orderly, precise, and balanced, objective statements of Christian faith. Other Reformed confessions are more discursive and are concerned with the experience of faith as well as its objective statement. The Scots Confession (1560) has been described as "the warm utterance of a people's heart." It states the Reformed faith in plain language, "revealing conviction, determination, and enthusiasm."[12] It is more pictorial and historical than abstract in style. As such it is in contrast with the Gallican Confession and the Belgic Confession.

In the 1580s, an attempt to prepare a Reformed confession fell through, and a compilation or harmony of Reformed creeds was substituted. This task was entrusted to Reformed theologians Beza, Daneau, and Salnar. They produced a harmony that included the Lutheran Augsburg Confession. This was later translated into English and published as a harmony of Reformed confessions in 1842.[13]

In the twentieth century, Karl Barth opposed the effort to write a universal Reformed creed. He defined a Reformed creed in this way: "A Reformed Creed is a statement, spontaneously and publicly formulated by a Christian community within a geographically limited area which, until further action, defines its character for outsiders; and which, until further action, gives guidance for its own doctrine and life; it is a formulation of the insight currently given to the whole Christian church by the revelation of God in Jesus Christ, witnessed to by Holy Scriptures alone."[14]

Creeds in the Seventeenth Century

The creeds of the seventeenth century continue but modify the creedal patterns of the sixteenth century. The sixteenth-century Protestant creeds were written by a church in crisis, in the heat of ecclesiastical and social change. They express the vibrance of the faith and the clarity of direction better than the subtle nuances of theology. The authors of the sixteenth-century creeds were primarily preachers, filled with a sense of urgency and often involved in polemical struggles. The theology of the seventeenth century had more of a school character. The confessions of the seventeenth century are distinguished by being built on 100 to 150 years of theological work. Hence their language has a precision and a clarity that is sometimes missing in the sixteenth-century confessions. In terms of technical theology, the Reformed confessions of the seventeenth century are masterpieces.

The confession and catechisms written by the Westminster Assembly (1643–1647) became the basic Reformed confession of English-speaking Presbyterians and, with revisions, of Congregationalists, and of many Baptists as well. This confession was written during the English civil war and reflects the Puritan theology of the period. It has all the virtues of a highly developed, precise, technically refined theology as well as the particular imprint of English Puritanism. Its virtues are also its weaknesses. In places it knows too much about God and God's will, and it lacks both the generosity of the Second Helvetic Confession and the personal and experiential warmth of the Scots and Second Helvetic Confessions. Yet its theological excellence is such that it virtually excluded all other confessions of faith from English-speaking Reformed churches for three centuries.

After the high-water mark of scholasticism in the seventeenth century, there was a decline in the writing of theology and in the writing of confessions. Battles over creedal subscription replaced the writing of creeds. Members of the Westminster Assembly had themselves strenuously opposed the imposition of creeds on the believing community. Yet a clear determination of the authority of creeds was difficult. In what sense are creeds a test of orthodoxy and of the authenticity of the community? English-speaking Presbyterians from the 1640s until the middle of the twentieth century debated, sometimes with great rancor, the authority of the Westminster Confession. The formulas specified that the Westminster Confession was to be accepted as containing the system of doctrine or the substance of doctrine as taught in the scriptures. This left undefined the meaning of "substance" or "system." One persuasive answer to this dilemma was given by Charles Hodge. In accepting the Westminster Confession, Hodge declared, the believer affirms that he or she is Christian, Protestant, and Reformed.[15]

Contemporary Creeds

Recent decades have seen a plethora of creedal formulas. Avery Dulles has written, "Probably no period in history has seen such a burgeoning of new creedal forms as our own."[16] Contemporary events and needs have called forth creeds in ways that contribute to their weakness as well as to their strength. *Reformed Witness Today: A Collection of Confessions and Statements of Faith*, issued by the World Alliance of Reformed Churches, contains thirty-three Reformed creeds, and this is not an exhaustive list.[17]

The need for individuals and communities caught up in the crisis of belief in our time to bring to expression their own faith or lack of faith has been one source of creeds. Robert Bilheimer has written, "The act of confession forces the person and the community to ever deeper levels of the authentic."[18] The writing of confessions does contribute to the church's examination of itself and to an understanding of its own crisis of faith. In this sense creedal statements today differ in their content significantly from the older creeds.

In addition to the crisis of faith within the church, modern creeds reflect the problems and crises of contemporary society. National Socialism in Germany called forth the Barmen Declaration. Communism likewise put the church at great risk. The threat of nuclear war, the new awareness of human dignity leading to an emphasis on human rights, the exploitation of the physical environment, the migration of people and the breakup of Christendom, the challenge to Western culture, the breakup of old established patterns of life—all have contributed to the writing of creeds. Hence most contemporary creeds have emphasized the human situation more explicitly and made social and cultural crises occasions of confession far more than did the traditional creeds.

This shift in focus to the human condition was also supported by the Enlightenment's concern for autonomy and by pietism in the church. Both placed an emphasis on subjectivity. In the modern world, theology began to be defined as reflection on believing experience. The result is that contemporary theologies as well as confessions become more expressivistic.

All creeds have reflected their social environment. The twentieth century is no exception. Contemporary culture is distinguished by its radical challenges to the faith, challenges that may strengthen but may also threaten the faith. Events in Germany, for example, in the 1930s became for some Christians the revelatory event, modifying the traditional Christian affirmation. In response the Confessing Church declared that in the church we listen only to Jesus Christ. Another example of the impact of the social situation in creedal writing today and a different approach is the confession of the Presbyterian-Reformed Church in Cuba. After the Cuban revolution, the church declared, "When the Marxists insist on the 'economical' as the basic element, fundamental for interpreting the significance of human life as it is developed in History, they make the Church—one of these ironies of History—reconsider the Biblical criterion of the human being as an 'econome.'"[19] The social context here is clearly elevated in importance, and the issue of the norm of faith is acutely raised. In contrast, the Barmen Declaration forthrightly began with the Word of God in the church and then sought to understand the world in the light of the revelation of God in Jesus Christ.

A Brief Statement of Faith: Presbyterian Church (U.S.A.)

Our brief review brings us to the present. The Presbyterian Church has always confessed its continuity with the people of God from Adam until today. It has also always known that it has had to live and confess the Christian faith in its own time and place. Today the Presbyterian Church (U.S.A.) attempts to do this by affirming the ancient creeds and confessions and by declaring the faith as best we can in the idiom, language, and experience of our time.

Today, as always, a Christian confession is the wisdom that makes sense out of life. It is the insight that enables us to put the disparate facts of human experience together in a coherent whole, in the light of God's revelation in Jesus Christ. Everyone lives by faith, a faith in the light of which the facts of life are evaluated and organized. "We believe in order to understand" who we are, who God is, and what the world is all about.

Augustine once said, "Love God and do as you please."

But Augustinians and Calvinists have also said, "Believe in God who has made himself known in Jesus Christ and think what you will." It is this faith which enables us to understand the world in all of its political, social, economic, and cultural expressions. The Christian confession bears witness to Christian faith as that which enables us to make more sense out of life, to find more meaning in life, and to see more clearly the significance of our common lives than does any other faith whatsoever.

"A Brief Statement of Faith: Presbyterian Church (U.S.A.)," therefore, does not intend to say what we think or how we feel or what we propose to do. It is an endeavor to proclaim the historical faith of the church (1) on the authority of scripture, (2) in fellowship with Christians who have confessed the faith through the centuries, and (3) in the idiom of our time. The committee that drafted this Statement was committed to catholicity: that is, it undertook to write a confession that the members of the church can confess with their hearts and with their minds. In the church generally and in Protestantism particularly, the authenticity of a confession is finally established not by the action of a council or a church court but by the approbation of the people of God, by the commonsense wisdom of the Christian community over a period of time. Or, to put it more theologically, a creed or confession is made authentic by the testimony of the Holy Spirit in the life of the church, not by an assembly vote. Hence the catholicity of the confession is critically important. It must arise out of life in the church as the believing community.

The catholicity of the confession means that a statement of faith must be for all Christians. A statement of faith may be occasional—that is, arising out of a particular situation—but a Christian confession of faith should never be just for some Christians. It must be written for all. Hence it is the intention of the committee that "A Brief Statement" should be a confession that the overwhelming majority of Christian people everywhere can confess.

The catholicity of a statement of faith means it is a confession for the church of all ages, for those who have lived and who are now the church triumphant, and for those who shall live in the future. This confession in the worship of the church must be confessed in company with all the hosts of heaven.

The committee to write "A Brief Statement" was diverse. The consequence of this diversity was five years of study, debate, struggle, and anguish. The Brief Statement is not necessarily what any one person would have written alone. It comes, like all creeds and confessions, out of the intense interaction of a diverse people. This means that it also comes authentically out of the life of the worshiping, believing community which is the church. The intention of the committee was to prepare a brief statement that was neither idiosyncratic nor trendy. Its purpose is to present a statement of the historic Christian, Protestant, and Reformed faith, under the authority of scripture in the light of the witness of the church in all ages and in the idiom of Christian witness in our time. The Brief Statement is intended to express what the church believes, confesses, and teaches. It is intended to join, albeit modestly, the tradition of statements of faith that have come before and that have served in their time and place.

Notes

1. In this article I have made use of my books *Creeds of the Churches*, 3rd ed. (Atlanta: John Knox Press, 1982), and *Introduction to the Reformed Tradition*, rev. ed. (Atlanta: John Knox Press, 1981).

2. Vernon H. Neufeld, *The Earliest Christian Confessions* (Grand Rapids: Wm. B. Eerdmans Publishing Co., 1964), p. 142.

3. Origen, *Exhortation to Martyrdom* 5, *Alexandrian Christianity*, ed. Henry Chadwick and J. E. L. Oulton, Library of Christian Classics, vol. 2 (Philadelphia: Westminster Press, 1954), p. 396.
4. Geoffrey Wainwright, *Doxology: The Praise of God in Worship, Doctrine, and Life* (New York: Oxford University Press, 1980).
5. Karl Barth, *Church Dogmatics* III/4 (Edinburgh: T. & T. Clark, 1961), pp. 73–86.
6. J. N. D. Kelly, *Early Christian Creeds*, 3rd ed. (New York: David McKay Co., 1972).
7. Karl Barth, *Church Dogmatics* IV/3, Part 2 (Edinburgh: T. & T. Clark, 1962), p. 866.
8. Kelly, *Early Christian Creeds*, p. 32.
9. Ibid., pp. 64–65. Cf. A. C. McGiffert, *The Apostles' Creed* (New York: Charles Scribner's Sons, 1902).
10. Some scholars argue that Luther sent the theses first to the bishops. Cf. Erwin Iserloh, "Martin Luther and the Coming of the Reformation," in *Reformation and Counter-Reformation*, ed. Hubert Jedin and John Dolan (New York: Crossroad Publishing Co., 1980), pp. 47–48.
11. Philip Schaff, *The Creeds of Christendom*, vol. 1 (New York: Harper & Brothers, 1877; reprint, Grand Rapids: Baker Book House, 1983), pp. 389–390.
12. Jenny Wormald, *Court, Kirk, and Community: Scotland, 1470–1625* (Toronto: University of Toronto Press, 1981), pp. 120ff.
13. Leith, *Creeds of the Churches*, pp. 128–129.
14. Karl Barth, *Theology and Church: Shorter Writings, 1920–1928* (New York: Harper & Row, 1962), p. 112.
15. Archibald Alexander Hodge, *A Commentary on the Confession of Faith* (Philadelphia: Presbyterian Board of Christian Education, 1869).
16. Avery Dulles, "Modern Credal Affirmations," in *Foundation Documents of the Faith*, ed. Cyril S. Rodd (Edinburgh: T. &. T. Clark, 1987), p. 125.
17. Lukas Vischer, *Reformed Witness Today* (Bern, 1982).
18. Robert Bilheimer, "Confessing Faith in God Today," *International Review of Missions* 67:148 (1948).
19. Vischer, *Reformed Witness Today*, p. 172.

The Ecumenical Significance of the Brief Statement of Faith 2

David Willis-Watkins

The Brief Statement of Faith intends to reconfess the catholic faith. In doing so, it makes claims that are of ecumenical significance. That significance comes partly from the way the Brief Statement of Faith reconfesses essentials of the faith that have already been received by the whole church in the earliest ecumenical councils. It is partly due, however, to its treatment of issues on which there has not been universal reception but which also belong to the future catholicity of the faith.

In this essay we will look at two features of the Brief Statement of Faith that are fresh confessions of ecumenically held belief (concerning the triune God and concerning the priority of grace), and we will look at two features that are stances which are not yet matters of ecumenical agreement (concerning new definitions of the "whole inhabited earth" whose care is enjoined on us by the gospel, and concerning the inclusiveness of the church's ministry). These two sets of features are mutually informing: Contemporary crises help shape the selection and treatment of ecumenically held doctrines to be reconfessed, and the new confessional stands are necessary implicates of the ancient faith newly confessed.

Belonging to the Triune God

Although it has some important ramifications for interchurch dialogues, the ecumenical character of the Brief Statement of Faith primarily derives from what it means to belong in life and in death to the one triune God. This particular belonging means believers' life together in the one holy catholic and apostolic church. And since the whole of creation, not just the church, also belongs to this God, the faith involves the church in worldly service. There are thus two senses of "ecumenical" which are rooted in the nature of God's embracing grace: the catholicity of the faith, and the worldly expression of that faith in joyful service to all God's creatures.

Neither of these senses of ecumenical is static. The reality in which they are grounded and to which they are a response is the life-giving and life-correcting love of the triune God. This reality is reconfessed and served innovatively in successive cultural contexts as the church is continually being reformed according to the Word in the power of the Spirit. That is why the forward movement of the confessing church throughout history is a matter of fresh reliance on the promises of the one living God who graciously refuses to be disposed of for convenience' sake, as opposed to the attractively portable user-friendly gods who charm us most. The psalmist contrasts the steadfastness of the living God with the lifelessness of the idols; but the point is also that people take on the characteristics of what they worship. "They [the idols] have hands, but do not feel; feet, but do not walk; and they do not make a sound in their throat. Those who make them are like them; so are all who trust in them. O Israel, trust in the LORD!" (Ps. 115:7–9a).

To distinguish between the living God and useful gods, we

are dependent on the history of God's fidelity as witnessed to in the scriptures, which are continually being reread and reinterpreted in the community of faith. The once-for-all character of God's definitive self-disclosure and saving action in Christ requires freshness of reconfession in the face of crises (which themselves are identified as crises in the light of the good news of God's love). God, definitively disclosed once-for-all, continues to encounter us in the present and will do so in the future. Fidelity to God is more than duplicating past events (as if that were possible); it is responding to God who calls us to new action in new times. Faithful response is a matter of memory and hope: the actively representative memory of God's prior fidelity, and the actively efficacious hope in the future of God's fidelity. This kind of memory and this kind of hope are the poles of the creative tension through which the living God works to continue reforming the church according to the Word by the power of the Spirit.

The trinitarian structure of the Brief Statement of Faith seeks to make clear the dynamic relation between the identity of the triune God and the identity-in-response of God's people. Lines 1–6 set out the underlying theme and the structure of the Brief Statement of Faith:

> In life and in death we belong to God.
>   Through the grace of our Lord Jesus Christ,
>   the love of God,
>   and the communion of the Holy Spirit,
>   we believe in the one triune God,
>   in whom alone we trust.

"In life and in death we belong to God." This opening line is intended to have a certain joyful starkness about it. It expresses the conviction of the people of the Old and New Testaments that we are who we are because of God's initiative. From among bands of aimless wanderers, God chose to call a people into being. Belonging to the living God reorders and judges other forms and experiences of belonging, some of which are idolatrous servitude. There is specificity in belonging to God in life and death. That is what the great Shema in Deuteronomy 5 and 6 is all about: "Hear, O Israel. I am the LORD your God, who brought you out of the land of Egypt, out of the house of bondage. You shall have no other gods before me" (Deut. 5:1, 6–7). The rest of the commandments are variations on this central point, that there are comforts and commitments which are integral to belonging to the living God.[1]

The confession made in this opening line is one of the strongest features of the tradition in which the Brief Statement of Faith stands. The opening question of the Heidelberg Catechism is resounding: "*Q. 1.* What is your only comfort, in life and in death? *A.* That I belong—body and soul, in life and in death—not to myself but to my faithful Savior, Jesus Christ, who at the cost of his own blood . . ." The full text of the answer of this question is worth pondering (*Book of Confessions*, 4.001). The first of the Barmen Declaration's "evangelical truths" is unmistakable on this point: "Jesus Christ, as he is attested for us in Holy Scripture, is the one Word of God which we have to hear and which we have to trust and obey in life and in death." The rest of this section of the Barmen Declaration lays the foundation for the statements concerning God's claim on our whole life and our grateful service to God's creatures (*Book of Confessions*, 8.10–.15).

It makes all the difference in the world—in the world, and not just in the church—which God it is that we belong to and trust and obey. Lines 2–6 are carefully constructed to make that as concisely clear as possible. Grammatically, the heart of that sentence is line 5 ("we believe in the one triune

God"); lines 2–4 ("Through the grace of our Lord Jesus Christ, the love of God, and the communion of the Holy Spirit") introduce the order of the apostolic benediction and declare how believing in the one triune God comes about; and line 6 ("in whom alone we trust") intends to make it clear that such believing is a matter of a trusting relationship that has a liberating focus.

Whatever else the documents in the *Book of Confessions* may be, they are trinitarian. This is true not only of the earliest creeds in it, the Nicene (Constantinopolitan) and the Apostles', but of the others as well. In its preface, the Confession of 1967 states that it does not intend to include all the traditional topics of theology, and then says: "For example, the Trinity and the Person of Christ are not redefined but are recognized and reaffirmed as forming the basis and determining the structure of the Christian faith" (*Book of Confessions*, 9.05). The controlling paragraph of the Confession of 1967 (9.07, called "The Confession") claims: "This work of God, the Father, Son, and Holy Spirit, is the foundation of all confessional statements about God, man, and the world." The opening chapter of the Scots Confession begins with a classical binding together of the existential character of faith and the identity of the God thus trusted and served:

> We confess and acknowledge one God alone, to whom alone we must cleave, whom alone we must serve, whom only we must worship, and in whom alone we put our trust. Who is eternal, infinite, immeasurable, incomprehensible, omnipotent, invisible; one in substance and yet distinct in three persons, the Father, the Son, and the Holy Ghost. (*Book of Confessions*, 3.01)

The Brief Statement of Faith does not use the language of one substance and three persons. Instead it draws on another term, "the one triune God," to make it as clear as possible that it is the same God who is being praised and confessed with an expanded range of images. That is a hallmark of the Brief Statement of Faith: It holds fast to the triune nature of God, and it seeks to express the faith with the more inclusive range of language which we are convinced this God—precisely this triune God—wills for our time.

The Brief Statement goes about speaking inclusively of the triune God in several ways. One has just been mentioned: using the designation "triune God" (which is also recommended as a contemporary usage by the 197th General Assembly (1985) in its Definitions and Guidelines on inclusive language with reference to God, *Minutes*, Part I: *Journal*, pp. 419–420). Another is to speak of God with imagery biblically associated with female and male activity (see lines 39–42) and by the use of line 25 ("whom Jesus called Abba, Father"). A third, and a structurally essential way, is by making it clear that it is the one God whose nature and activity are being confessed in each section of the Brief Statement (lines 7–23, 24–42, 43–64). That is, the parallel in each section is intentional: "We trust in Jesus Christ, fully God, fully human. . . . We trust in God, whom Jesus called Abba, Father. . . . We trust in God the Holy Spirit . . ." And, finally, the trinitarian Gloria, which uses the baptismal formula, is retained in the doxology of line 68. Its location here means that it comes after examples of inclusive language and yet is kept as part of what joins us to other branches of the church universal. This retention is also in keeping with the 1985 General Assembly's guidelines on gender language.[2]

The Brief Statement of Faith is of ecumenical significance in that it reconfesses the universal church's trust in the triune God, and does so in ways that both reaffirm our unity with the rest of the church and are inclusive in the range of imagery used. The doctrine of the triune God functions here to identify the God to whom the whole of creation belongs. It also functions to provide the structure within which other affirmations are properly treated, including the priority of grace.

The Priority of Grace

Christian freedom is the practice of responding in all things to God's initiative. There is an order to this grace-full living: who God is, therefore who God's people are; how Christ has welcomed us, therefore how we are to welcome others; how God has reconciled the world to Godself, therefore how we are to live out that reconciliation in every area. The Brief Statement insists on this order of grace, and in doing so it is reclaiming one of the emphases that historically the Reformed tradition has sought to keep vital for the sake of the whole church.

In this insistence on the priority of grace, the Reformed teaching is part of a larger and ancient tradition. Luther's breakthrough for the sake of the catholicity of the church was itself a rediscovery of Pauline and Augustinian theology, which had countless representatives throughout the centuries. It is a badly impoverished reading of church history and of medieval culture, in the West and the East, to suggest that before the Reformation the church taught that ultimately people are saved otherwise than by grace—however attenuated definitions of grace had often indeed become. Nonetheless, there was a certain thoroughness with which Calvin sought to spell out the implications of "by grace alone" for the whole of life—not just for the personal life of the forgiven sinner, but for the social structure in which the faithful community lives. In any event, there has been a rather characteristic Reformed ethos that has struggled to maintain the ordering priority of grace (and there is something of Reformed irony in struggling by the grace of God to live by grace!).

This relentless prominence given to wholeness by grace

alone has, until recently, characterized (and, by God's mercy, will again characterize) the evangelical churches. It is the precision of the Barmen Declaration on the priority of grace that made it, and makes it, such a scandalously prophetic word. The second "evangelical truth" in Barmen deals explicitly with grace and consequences.

> As Jesus Christ is God's assurance of the forgiveness of all our sins, so in the same way and with the same seriousness he is also God's mighty claim upon our whole life. Through him befalls us a joyful deliverance from the godless fetters of this world for a free, grateful service to his creatures.
>
> We reject the false doctrine, as though there were areas of our life in which we would not belong to Jesus Christ, but to other lords—areas in which we would not need justification and sanctification through him. (*Book of Confessions*, 8.14–.15)

Any document that claims to be in continuity with evangelical catholicity, and to be a fresh expression thereof, and of the Reformed tradition more particularly, must reconfess the good news of God's utterly unmerited favor, utterly undeserved forgiveness, utterly freeing activity for empowering the new life intended for all God's creatures. This priority of grace is reconfessed in the Brief Statement not simply by the section on the new life, but above all, again, by the structure of the document.

One could treat the major affirmations of the faith in any of a number of orders, and in fact the documents in the *Book of Confessions* reflect that flexibility. Perhaps the one most frequently used is that of the Nicene and Apostles' Creeds: Father, Son, Holy Spirit. There are advantages to that more traditional sequence; for example, the goodness of creation and the seriousness of human rebellion are shown as the background for understanding the significance of Christ's person and work, and for understanding the significance of the Holy Spirit in applying the benefits of Christ to enable the new life together.

The Brief Statement of Faith, however, follows the sequence: Christ, Father-Abba, Holy Spirit. It does so partly because that is the order of the apostolic benediction. However, it also does so to make a point about the direction or movement of the trusting relationship out of which the church can dare make such bold—even outlandishly scandalous—claims about God in our fragmented and suffering world. For others it may be different; but for the Christian community it is mainly (not exclusively, but mainly) because of the experience of deliverance that we are able to say something about the benevolence of God as Creator and about the dynamics of the new life in the Spirit. This is a recurrent theme in Reformed theology: the goodness of the image of God in which we were created is known from its restoration. That restoration in all its inclusive dynamic and direction for the whole of creation is known and practiced, with daily repentance and forgiveness, in the community equipped by the Spirit to share in Christ's own ongoing ministry. Each section is internally ordered to reflect the grace-response sequence. If this internal sequence were missed, the priority of grace would be obscured and we would have on our hands a document of pretentious works righteousness. As it is, however, the final section (beginning at line 65) accurately reinforces the firm joy and seasoned faith intended to be expressed by this document.

The Brief Statement of Faith is of ecumenical significance in that it reconfesses the priority of grace to which earlier creeds and confessions also adhere, and does so in ways that acknowledge the cost of discipleship and affirm the sovereignty of God's love. The sequence of grace-response functions in each section to point to what belonging to the triune God means in all things, including the present ecological crisis.

The Ecology of the New Life

Part of the urgency behind the Brief Statement is the conviction that the church must take a confessing stand about the ecological crisis.

It is not a new thing to acknowledge that all creation belongs to God or that Christian stewardship involves a responsibility toward creation. But a thoroughly altered understanding of responsibility toward the rest of creation is called for in the face of two dimensions of the problem. The first is the actual spoliation of the environment. The second is the remarkable tenacity (even among those who recognize the problem) of priorities that continue to operate when we assign to others the sacrifices needed for the earth's health.

There is obviously a growing recognition of the extent to which humanity is proving capable of consuming the natural environment. It was not so long ago that the nonhuman portion of creation could be treated as an entity that was inexhaustible and that existed for humanity's well-being. The extent of deforestation, of air and water pollution, of defacing the planet, or depleting the earth's deep resources is astounding. There is understandable confusion over the technology and political realism involved in dealing with the global complexities of the ecological crisis—fair enough. But the appalling extent of the damage done the environment is matched by the extent to which most of us seem to acknowledge these crises as conditions whose causes and solutions are somebody else's responsibility.

In the structure of the Brief Statement, this is addressed following the confession of God's sovereign love in creating the world good. The goodness of the world—because created by the good God to whom all things belong—is the background for what follows, namely our complicity in that which resists God's love. Our share in the ecological crisis is named as part of the death-dealing rebellion against this God of sovereign love. "But we rebel against God: refusing to love God and neighbor, corrupting ourselves, exploiting others, and threatening death to the planet entrusted to our care. We deserve God's judgment. Yet God rules with justice and mercy to redeem creation" (lines 30–36). The final word is not about the power of sin, or about our deserving God's judgment—accurate and necessary as the penultimate word may be. The final word is about God's fidelity, about God's forgiveness which frees us to live transforming lives (lines 54–59), about God's new heaven and new earth for which we actively wait. "In gratitude to God we strive to serve Christ in our daily tasks and to live holy and joyful lives, even as we watch for God's new heaven and new earth, praying, 'Come, Lord Jesus!'" (lines 60–64).

Of ecumenical significance on this issue is the way the Brief Statement of Faith: (a) reflects what is by now the concern of the contemporary church, around the world and in every culture, with the ecological crisis; (b) lifts this global concern, expressed at many levels, to the level of confessional status; (c) does so in the form of a conviction of our complicity in the ecological crisis as part of the sin for which we deserve God's judgment; and (d) makes sure that the final word we confess is that of the extent of God's ultimate rule, which includes the redemption of creation, and which frees us for grateful service in that cause.

The Inclusiveness of the Church's Ministry

This heading—the inclusiveness of the church's ministry—does not accurately enough express the particular newness with which the Brief Statement of Faith applies the already received catholic faith to the nature of the ministry. It is not new to confess that the ministry is not technically the church's, but Christ's own ongoing ministry through the church. It is not new to confess that this ministry is carried out through all those who are baptized into Christ. It is not new to confess that the ministry is inclusive in the sense that it belongs to the priesthood of all believers, regardless of race, age, class, gender, health. What is new is to make it a matter of confessional status that women and men are called to all ministries of the church. This means that there is no office in the church from which women who are gifted and equipped by the Spirit for that office are to be excluded, if the fullness of Christ's own ongoing ministry is to be even more faithfully shared by forgiven sinners in the future than in the past.

What is at stake here is not simply the status of women in the church, though that is part of it, and not simply the appallingly overdue correction of injustice done people because of their gender, though that correction would be reason enough for this confessional stand. At stake is what constitutes a greater fullness of the ministry of the catholic church, including all forms of the special ministry of the Word through preaching and sacrament and all forms of governance. This has the significance of calling all churches to a more fully catholic ministry, that is, one which is inclusive throughout all structures of the church. It makes one of the marks of a more fully catholic ministry that consecration to every office of ministry be open to forgiven sinners—regardless of their gender—who are gifted and equipped by the Spirit for that office.

The imperative for this stand arises from the indicative, once again, of who God is and what it means to belong to God. The fundamental reasons for a more fully catholic ministry derive from the trinitarian character of the faith—nothing less. Note the lines (48–53) of the Brief Statement that deal with this stand, and note their relation to the structure of the rest of the document.

The same Spirit
who inspired the prophets and apostles
rules our faith and life in Christ through Scripture,

baptizes us in living water,
feeds us with the bread of life,
and calls women and men to all ministries of the church.

The reign of God proclaimed by Jesus, and the benefits of his death and resurrection, include breaking the power of sin and evil and delivering us from death to life eternal (lines 22–23). This establishing of justice applies to the freeing activity of God by which all forms of oppression are exposed and combated. Those who are equally forgiven, renewed, freed are also equally created in God's image to live in one community—and this comes about because of God's sovereign love. "In sovereign love God created the world good and makes everyone, male and female, of every race and people, equally in God's image to live as one community" (lines 26–29). All who experience the benefits of redemption and the goodness of being created in God's image are also those who are bound together by the Spirit in the body of Christ. This is the body of those who by the Spirit are inspired and encouraged and ruled through scripture to be an effective sign, in a broken and fearful world, of the wholeness God intends for all people (lines 48–59). The whole church is called to a more fully catholic ministry, one that is inclusive of those who share equally in the holiness of life in the Spirit.

This stand on the future of the ministry of the catholic church is not taken in isolation from other partners in dialogue but comes about as part of the Presbyterian Church's commitment to ecumenical relations. Early drafts of the Brief Statement were, for example, shared with official bodies of other denominations and their critical suggestions were invited. It is clear that there are still deep and painful divisions among Christians—especially on the nature of the ministry. The conflict over this issue is more painful among those denominations which share with us a high doctrine of the ministry. Those are the ecumenical partners with whom we must above all persevere in hearing and speaking in love.

Presbyterians have traditionally placed a high value on the ministry of the Word through preaching and sacrament, and tend to maintain a relatively high educational standard as one of the things meant by a person's being gifted and equipped by the Spirit for the special ministry of the Word. That is mainly because Presbyterians take seriously the apostolic succession of the gospel. They see theological education as a part of what enables persons critically to think through the faith and engage in the processes by which the church remains the confessing congregation of the faithful. This is a process in which the voices of other Christian traditions are necessary. Every confessing act is costly, and this stand on the inclusive nature of all forms of the church's ministry is not taken lightly—or taken as if one part of the body of Christ could suffer without affecting every other part. The cost of discipleship is eventually shared by all in the body of Christ as new demands of the gospel are joyfully heeded.

Notes

1. See 1 Cor. 6:19, and Calvin's commentary on that passage, in *Calvin: Institutes of the Christian Religion*, ed. J. T. McNeill, tr. Ford Lewis Battles (Philadelphia: Westminster Press, 1960), vol. 1, p. 690.

2. "The Trinitarian designation, 'Father-Son-Holy Spirit,' is an ancient creedal formula and as such should not be altered. It is deeply rooted in our theological tradition, is shared widely by the church catholic, and is basic to many of our ecumenical relationships. It is not theologically acceptable to refer to the persons of the Trinity in terms of function alone. . . . While the language of the Trinitarian formula should remain unchanged, we must still remember that this formula is not the only way by which we refer to God, and that efforts to express the fullness of our knowledge of God in terms of being and function are to be encouraged." Guideline 2.c, *Minutes of the 197th General Assembly of the Presbyterian Church (U.S.A.), 1985*, Part I: *Journal*, para. 32.012, p. 420.

Contemporary Confession and Biblical Authority 3

William C. Placher

Few questions matter as much for the confession of our faith today as the way we treat the authority and interpretation of the Bible. This has always been an important topic for Reformed Christians, of course; it even provides the starting point for some of our classic confessions. But it assumes particular importance today because it sets some of the crucial dividing lines in contemporary American Christianity.

Robert Wuthnow's fine book *The Restructuring of American Religion* (1988) reminds us that as recently as a generation ago denominational lines defined the critical divisions for American Christians. In the years just after World War II, a Presbyterian General Assembly condemned the "cultic worship of Mary" among Catholics, and Cardinal Spellman denounced Protestant critics of Catholicism as "unhooded Klansmen." Debates among Protestant bodies were usually less sharp, but Presbyterians, Lutherans, Baptists, and others sometimes still attacked each other with vigor. Most Christians, according to the best sociological data, had been reared in a single denomination, seldom switched to another, and knew very little about the beliefs and practices of other denominations.[1]

How dramatically things have changed! In an ecumenical age, we have abandoned the old polemics. In many Presbyterian churches—and in this we are not unique—a majority of the members were not brought up as Presbyterians. Denominational boundaries seem to be fading. It does not follow, however, that American Christians have turned into one big happy family. If we rarely denounce other denominations, some conservative preachers often enough still excoriate "liberals" or "secular humanists," and attacks on "fundamentalists" or "TV evangelists" regularly sound from some more liberal pulpits. *Those* are the lines along which we feel most bitterly divided these days, and the authority of scripture often seems the crucial dividing issue. It follows that, if contemporary American Christians pick up a statement of faith wanting to know "What is it that *we* believe," they may well be more concerned about this question than about traditional confessional debates over, say, the sacraments or justification.

When we ask about the authority of the Bible these days, however, I think we are apt to make a big mistake. We tend to cast the question purely in terms of "How much authority does the Bible have?" A little? A lot? A fair amount? Scarcely any? Total and complete? It is as if we want to rank people on a single scale, with scores from 1 to 100.[2]

That way of posing the question distorts the issue. We cannot rank people's beliefs about the authority of scripture along such a single scale, because scripture can function—and function powerfully—as authority for Christians in a number of different ways. There is not just one model for *really* taking the authority of the Bible seriously. I want, in fact, to describe three such models, argue that each of them has solid antecedents in the Reformed tradition, and then draw some conclusions about what this should mean for our contemporary practice and confession of faith.

Three Models of Biblical Authority

I propose that the Bible can function as authority in our lives as Christians (1) as a set of true propositions, (2) as a transforming word, or (3) as the narrative of God's identity.[3]

1. Scripture can function authoritatively as true propositions. "The Bible," Charles Hodge wrote over a century ago in the greatest formulation of Princeton orthodoxy, "is to the theologian what nature is to the man of science. It is his storehouse of facts. . . . Inspiration extends to all the contents. . . . It is not confined to moral and religious truths, but extends to the statement of facts, whether scientific, historical, or geographical. . . . It extends to everything which any sacred writer asserts to be true."[4]

Hodge's position was a complex one. He rejected the "mechanical theory of inspiration"; he acknowledged that the prophets "were not like calculating machines which grind out logarithms with infallible correctness."[5] He distinguished the *opinions* the biblical authors may have had from what they *taught*, maintaining that only the latter was authoritative for Christian faith. Thus, for instance, the author of the book of Joshua evidently *believed* that the sun moves around the earth, and he *assumed* as much when he described the sun as standing still, but he did not *teach* it, and therefore, Hodge thought, Christians need not believe it.[6]

Yet with all these careful qualifications, the basic model remains: we may have to understand the propositions of the Bible in context; we may not want to accept all the propositions in the Bible, but only those which constitute its teaching—but there are propositions in the Bible that are true, and we accept the authority of scripture when we accept their truth. Those who speak of the Bible as "infallible," "inerrant," or "verbally inspired" (terms that may or may not mean the same thing, depending on how they are used) usually take such a model for granted.

2. Consider, by way of contrast, how scripture might function authoritatively as transforming word. Remember how, in the third century, Antony heard a sermon on the text, "If you would be perfect, go, sell what you possess and give to the poor, and you will have treasure in heaven." So he went and sold, and spent the next seventy years or so in prayer and fasting in the desert.[7] We do not know anything about Antony's theory of biblical authority. His biographer emphasizes the saint's distaste for books and schoolwork from earliest childhood; and he grew up in third-century Egypt, with its tradition of allegorical interpretation. So it seems unlikely that Antony worried overmuch about the literal truth of every scriptural proposition—and yet it would seem odd to say that the Bible was less an authority in his life; it transformed him, forever.[8]

It may seem a huge jump from Antony to Rudolf Bultmann. We tend to think of Antony as a great ascetic but of Bultmann as a great skeptic: the apostle of demythologizing, a twentieth-century theologian who denied we could know much about the historical Jesus. But there is another side to Bultmann. He repeatedly affirmed that the life of authentic faith is the solution to the riddle of human existence and that such faith is possible only in response to the action of God in Jesus Christ. "Faith only became possible at a definite point in history in consequence of an *event*—viz., the event of Christ."[9] And we encounter that event when we hear of it in the Bible and in Christian preaching.

That is, in its way, a strong doctrine of the authority of scripture. The kerygma, the essential preaching of the gospel, encounters us only by way of the Bible, and hearing and accepting that kerygma is essential to living human life as it ought to be lived. Like a whole generation of theologians influenced by existentialism,[10] Bultmann emphasized the authority of that kerygmatic word by insisting that any attempt to buttress it by appeal to evidence—for example, of the historical accuracy of the Bible—only weakens and distorts faith. "The man who wishes to believe in God as his God must realize that he has nothing in his hand on which to base his faith. He is suspended in mid-air, and cannot demand a proof of the Word which addresses him."[11] You hear the Word, and its news of a gracious God transforms your life. It speaks with authority.

Many liberation theologians also understand scripture as above all a word that transforms. James Cone, for instance, has noted, "Black people in America had great confidence in the holy Book." Contemporary historical criticism of scripture, he continues, has not affected that confidence.

> This does not mean that black people are fundamentalists in the strict sense of the term. They have not been preoccupied with definitions of inspiration and infallibility. . . . It is as if blacks have intuitively drawn the all-important distinction between infallibility and reliability. They have not contended for a fully explicit infallibility, feeling perhaps that there is mystery in the Book, as there is in the Christ. What they have testified to is the Book's reliability: how it is the true and basic source for discovering the truth of Jesus Christ. . . . The authority of the Bible for Christology, therefore, does not lie in its objective status as the literal Word of God. Rather, it is found in its power to point to the One whom the people have met in the historical struggle for freedom. . . . Through the reading of Scripture . . . they are taken from the present to the past and then thrust back into their contemporary history with divine power to transform the sociopolitical context.[12]

In empowering oppressed people to transform their world, the Bible speaks with an authority that stands apart from claims about the truth of its individual propositions.

3. In saying that scripture can also function as authority by narrating God's identity—by telling stories that enable us to know who God is—I have particularly in mind an interpretation of the theology of Karl Barth developed by Hans Frei before his recent, untimely death. Frei's Yale colleague George Lindbeck has christened this general approach "postliberal theology."[13] But much of the recent work on literary approaches to scripture follows similar lines of thought.

Frei's argument goes roughly like this: As one reads the Gospel narratives, one is struck by their general casualness as to detail. As one reads the Gospels and compares them one with another, the chronologies and the geography do not even seem consistent. Moreover, one senses that their authors would not have been much disturbed had someone pointed out the inconsistencies. Such details are somehow not what these texts are *about*.

At the same time, suppose someone says, "The point of these stories is simply to draw general lessons about how human life should be lived. Whether there really was a person named Jesus, and what sort of person he was—that doesn't matter to the meaning of these narratives." That seems wrong somehow. The Gospels seem to be telling about an unsubstitutable person, Jesus of Nazareth, and claiming that who he was, and what he did, makes all the difference to who we are and what we can hope—just as the Old Testament delineates through story the character of the God who will become incarnate in Christ.

Much of scripture, in other words, functions like a vivid personal anecdote.[14] With such stories, we will often not vouch for the truth of the details, but sometimes the story captures something about the character of the person it describes in a way that nothing but a well-told story could. "You want to know what Grandfather was like," we say. "Well, I don't know if things really happened quite this way, but this story gets at the sort of person he was better than anything else I could say." So, too, it is not that the historical details are always accurate—as I said, scripture seems often casual in these matters—nor is it just that an individual passage seizes our attention and challenges our lives. Rather, the shape of the biblical stories as a whole pictures a world in which a character they call "God" is at work, and invites us to recognize how that world is in fact the world in which we live, and that God is indeed at work here. When we do recognize this, accepting the biblical world as our world and the God whose character emerges in their tales as our God, we are acknowledging the authority of scripture. Indeed, those who favor this model would argue that if we took the biblical stories as attempts at detailed, accurate history, we would be *distorting* their meaning and would therefore be *less* faithful to their authority.

Antecedents in the Reformed Tradition

Having set out these three ways in which the Bible can function as authority, I do not want to vote for one of the three as "the right answer." Rather, I first want to say that all three can lay claim to antecedents in our Reformed tradition.

1. "There is no question," as John Leith correctly observes, "that the authors of the [Westminster] Confession believed that the Bible was inspired and that God revealed himself in propositions."[15] By the Holy Spirit, they declared, "all the writers of the Holy Scriptures [were] inspired to record infallibly the mind and will of God," with "the Old Testament in Hebrew . . . and the New Testament in Greek . . . being immediately inspired by God." Somewhat more cautiously, the Second Helvetic Confession had earlier asserted that in Holy Scripture we have "the most complete exposition of all that pertains to a saving faith, and also to the framing of a life acceptable to God; and in this respect it is expressly com-

manded by God that nothing be either added to or taken from the same."[16]

Still, from its beginning the Reformed tradition has recognized that our faith does not rest on the truth of every proposition in the Bible. The Gospels were not written, Calvin admitted, "in such a manner, as to preserve, on all occasions, the exact order of time."[17] "We know that the Evangelists were not very exact as to the order of dates, or even in detailing minutely everything that Christ said or did."[18] Moreover, "when passages of Scripture are taken up at random, and no attention is paid to the context, we need not wonder that mistakes . . . frequently arise."[19]

Calvin therefore encouraged using the best scholarly tools of his time to understand the Bible better, and he emphasized that particular passages cannot simply be taken as isolated propositions but have to be understood in context. Those who followed him generally agreed on both points. Correct interpretation of the scriptures, the Second Helvetic Confession declares, will take into account "the nature of the language in which they were written" and "the circumstances in which they were set down" as well as expounding particular passages "in the light of like and unlike passages and of many and clearer passages" and seeking meanings "which agree with the rule of faith and love." The Westminster Confession acknowledges that "all things in Scripture are not alike plain in themselves" and therefore advises that "when there is a question about the true and full sense of any Scripture . . . it may be searched and known by other places that speak more clearly."[20]

Like Calvin and the authors of the other confessions of the Reformation period, the writers of the Westminster standards did not make use of the methods of modern critical history—those methods had not yet been invented!—and they said things about the authority and interpretation of scripture which are incompatible with those methods. On the other hand, they urged the use of the best scholarly methods of *their* day in interpreting scripture. They therefore left us an ambiguous heritage.[21] Those who reject many modern critical methods can cite relevant passages from the Reformation confessions. Those who say we should use the best scholarly methods of *our* day to understand the Bible can cite their precedent. The Confession of 1967, for instance, continues a Reformed tradition of commitment to careful biblical scholarship in a new context when it declares:

> The Scriptures, given under the guidance of the Holy Spirit, are nevertheless the words of men, conditioned by the language, thought forms, and literary fashions of the places and times at which they were written. They reflect views of life, history, and the cosmos which were then current. The church, therefore, has an obligation to approach the Scriptures with literary and historical understanding.[22]

In the conclusion of this essay, I will suggest that this ambiguous inheritance generates a tension we can best resolve by recognizing the legitimate place of more than one model of biblical authority.

2. The idea that scripture functions authoritatively in its power to transform our lives also has a solid Reformed background. For Westminster, after all, the first function of scripture is "to be the rule of faith and life." For the earlier Second Helvetic Confession, the scriptures teach "true wisdom and godliness, the reformation and government of churches; as also instruction in all duties of piety."[23] From the start, the Reformed tradition had emphasized the *practical* implications of scripture: what they imply for our lives and how we live them. "The Scripture," Calvin had written, "is not given us to satisfy our foolish curiosity or to serve our ambition. But it is useful, St. Paul tells us; and why? To teach us good doctrine, to console us, exhort us and render us perfect in

every good work. So to that use let us put it."[24] With its characteristic personal emphasis, the Heidelberg Catechism stated that "true faith" is not simply a matter of "certain knowledge by which I accept as true all that God has revealed to us in his Word, but also a wholehearted trust . . . that . . . to me also God has given the forgiveness of sins, everlasting righteousness and salvation."[25] The emphasis falls on the transformation of one's life.[26]

Furthermore, one of the most important themes of the Reformation accounts of scriptural authority is the role of the inward illumination of the Holy Spirit. We cannot come to Christ, the Second Helvetic Confession declares, "unless the Holy Spirit inwardly illumines" us. The authors of Westminster acknowledged "the inward illumination of the Spirit of God to be necessary for the saving understanding of such things as are revealed in the Word."[27] This means that correct interpretation cannot be simply a matter of understanding the truth of scriptural propositions. As we read the Word, the Spirit must also seize our hearts.

3. In qualifying the place of the first two models in the Reformed tradition, I have already indicated how scripture has functioned as authority by narrating God's identity. Perhaps the best way to summarize the point is by emphasizing the word "witness." The Confession of 1967 described the scriptures as "the witness without parallel" to "the one sufficient revelation of God . . . Jesus Christ, the Word of God incarnate." Barmen, earlier in the century, had captured roughly the same idea, with an echo of the sixteenth-century Heidelberg Catechism: "Jesus Christ, as he is attested for us in Holy Scripture, is the one Word of God which we have to hear and which we have to trust and obey in life and in death."[28] The Bible does not say, "Believe in the Bible." It says, "Believe in the gracious God revealed in Jesus Christ." It attests. It witnesses. It points beyond itself.

What it points to is this God in whom we are to put our

trust. As passages I quoted earlier indicated, Calvin and other early figures in our Reformed tradition conceded that the Bible was not always accurate as to details of chronology and other matters. But they would never have conceded that it could be inaccurate about the character of the God in whom we believe. In that sense, the meaning of much of the text is to tell us through story the identity of God.

Some Contemporary Applications

If there are different ways in which scripture can function as authority for Christians—at least some of those ways open to a strong sense of authority, without one of them being clearly "more committed to authority" than another—and if those different ways have sound antecedents in the Reformed tradition, it follows that we cannot pick one of them as "the only right answer." We therefore cannot rank everyone on a single scale of "how much" he or she believes in the authority of the Bible. We have to respect differences that are not matters of "more" or "less" but are simply "different."

Moreover, each of the three approaches I have mentioned stands incomplete by itself. An exclusive emphasis on the authority of the Bible as residing in the truth of its propositions risks turning Christian faith into a matter of pure intellectualism and chronic anxiety. The Reformed tradition has always emphasized that faith is not merely a matter of "certain knowledge" but also involves that "wholehearted trust" which is the gift of the Holy Spirit. Belief in the authority of scripture does not mean simply accepting a set of propositions as true but must include letting our lives be transformed as we encounter the God whom the Bible presents to us. Moreover, from the start, our Reformed tradition has acknowledged that our faith need not be bound to the accuracy of (for instance) every chronological or geographical detail of scripture. Yet if the authority of the Bible lies in the truth of propositions, every such concession begins to feel like an admission of defeat, a step on a slippery slope that leads away from faith. If we remember that scripture can also function powerfully in other ways, such awareness can at that point serve as a corrective and reassurance.

Those who think of scripture primarily as transforming word also have lessons to learn from other approaches. The Bible can transform us authentically only if it tells us something true. After all, it is only because God has acted that we can appropriately respond; otherwise we would be claiming to save ourselves rather than trusting in God's grace. So we need to know something—something true—about what God has done. Moreover, it is only because the *content* of the biblical narratives tells us something about the God in whom we believe that we can know that we are believing in God and not some idol of our own imagining.[29]

Finally, those who think of the Bible primarily as the narrative that portrays God's identity need to remember that they cannot avoid propositional truth claims altogether. An anecdotal account can help us to know who God is without accuracy as to many details, but there come points—crucifixion and resurrection might seem examples—where Christian faith cannot take a particular episode simply as an illustrative example. There we find ourselves needing to say, If God is what we believe God to be, then this really happened.[30] It is also the case that propositional truth and transforming power seem easier to explain to an ordinary congregation than matters of narrative structure and literary form. From earliest childhood, "Tell me the *stories* of Jesus" is one of the themes of our faith. And yet, perhaps because scientific methods dominate so much of our culture, the application of literary analysis to the Bible, rather than seeming simply a tool to help us understand what the text means, often arouses suspicions that we are somehow avoiding the real issue.[31] Those whose primary adherence is to this model need to find ways to make it more vivid in the life of the church.[32]

In short, we all need to learn from one another. What does that imply for the role of a contemporary statement of faith? First, such a statement ought not to take one particular theory of the authority of scripture—one of these three models or some other—and christen it "the correct" Presbyterian view on such matters. Here our tradition has had room for pluralism from the start, and we need to preserve it. We need to call people to take the authority of the Bible seriously and yet to remember that there are several ways of doing so.

Beyond that, I have regularly emphasized how the Bible can *function* as authority in the life of Christian people. It may be that the most important question about a contemporary statement of faith and the authority of scripture is not what the statement *says* on this topic but how it might *function* in the life of the church to encourage more serious study of the Bible. The problem of "biblical illiteracy" in our churches is generally acknowledged. When the average Christian—or even the average pastor—does not know the Bible very well, that sets limits on how we can use it as an authority. Too often, when we face controversial issues, the only language we have in which to discuss them is the language of contemporary politics—which often divides and angers us. We do not share a language of Christian categories in which to talk about things that matter to us. As stated in a resource document for the 1982 General Assembly of the United Presbyterian Church U.S.A., "One cannot expect to use the Bible in a positive way for guidance and direction in the midst of controversy if one is not accustomed to using it for guidance and direction in daily lives, both individually and corporately."[33] Moreover, when we do not know the Bible well, then, confronted with a particular passage, we too often have a choice between either accepting that passage in isolation as "true"—as a kind of proof text—or else simply deciding that we do not accept the authority of the Bible in this matter.

Many of our forebears knew scripture far better than we do. That enabled them to talk about the "truth" of scripture in sophisticated ways: keeping context in mind, weighing one passage against another, seeing a larger pattern. Too often, we just do not know enough to engage in that kind of interpretation. We do not know the Bible well enough to enable it to transform our lives. We have not immersed ourselves in the rich web of narrative that images a world and narrates the identity of God; we have not made its world our world.

If a contemporary statement of faith could be used often enough in worship to enter the life of our church as a common language and thus invite and open paths for further biblical study, that might be the single most important contribution it could make to our interpretation of the authority of scripture. To quote a position statement that emerged from the former Presbyterian Church U.S., "The Church needs always to remember that the use of Holy Scripture is more important than debates about its authority."[34] As our church debates the proposed new statement of faith, its cross-references to the Bible and the *Book of Confessions* may prove of particular educational value. It may be worth considering the possibility that its *usefulness* in liturgy and in Christian education are the most important contributions this Statement can make to the authority of the Bible in the life of our church.

Notes

1. Robert Wuthnow, *The Restructuring of American Religion* (Princeton, N.J.: Princeton University Press, 1988), pp. 73–79. Wuthnow cites the Lynds' data from "Middletown" in the 1920s, but his point is that little had changed even in the 1950s.

2. Such a tendency somewhat mars the otherwise excellent resource document of the 1982 General Assembly of the United Presbyterian Church U.S.A., "Biblical Authority and Interpretation" (see note 33). In the questions posed to the Presbyterian Panel in preparing that document, and even in the three models it proposes for understanding the authority of scripture, the terms used seem code words for different *quantities* of authority rather than different ways in which scripture could be authoritative—equally authoritative, or at least not neatly open to ranking. This is less true of the models offered in Donald K. McKim, *What Christians Believe About the Bible* (Nashville: Thomas Nelson Publishers, 1984).

3. David Kelsey seems to have thought about these issues more clearly and insightfully than anyone else I know. What follows owes much to his work, though I have diverged from and certainly simplified his conclusions. He identifies the following ways in which scripture can function as authority: its doctrines, its concepts, its narrative, its presentation of the identity of an agent, its images, its symbols, and its presentation of a form of self-understanding. See David H. Kelsey, *The Uses of Scripture in Recent Theology* (Philadelphia: Fortress Press, 1975).

4. Charles Hodge, *Systematic Theology*, vol. 1 (New York: Charles Scribner's Sons, 1872; reprint, Grand Rapids: Wm. B. Eerdmans Publishing Co., 1960), pp. 10, 163.

5. Ibid., pp. 156–157.

6. Ibid., p. 170. For a similarly nuanced view from a contemporary evangelical theologian, see Clark H. Pinnock, "How I Use the Bible in Doing Theology," in Robert K. Johnston, ed., *The Use of the Bible in Theology: Evangelical Options* (Atlanta: John Knox Press, 1985), p. 18.

7. Athanasius (?), *Life of Antony*, in *Nicene and Post-Nicene*

Fathers, 2nd series, vol. 4 (Grand Rapids: Wm. B. Eerdmans Publishing Co., 1957), p. 196.

8. See also Augustine's account of his conversion (in which the story of Antony played a crucial role) in *The Confessions*, tr. Rex Warner (New York: New American Library, Mentor-Omega Books, 1963), pp. 182–183.

9. Rudolf Bultmann, "New Testament and Mythology," in Hans Werner Bartsch, ed., *Kerygma and Myth*, tr. Reginald H. Fuller, rev. ed. (New York: Harper & Row, 1961), p. 22. See also Rudolf Bultmann, "Die Krisis des Glaubens," *Glauben und Verstehen*, vol. 2 (Tübingen: J. C. B. Mohr [Paul Siebeck], 1952), p. 16.

10. See also, for instance, Paul Tillich, *The Dynamics of Faith* (New York: Harper & Brothers, 1958), p. 34.

11. Rudolf Bultmann, "Bultmann Replies to His Critics," in Bartsch, ed., *Kerygma and Myth*, p. 211. The passage echoes Kierkegaard. See Søren Kierkegaard, *Philosophical Fragments*, tr. David F. Swenson, 2nd ed. (Princeton, N.J.: Princeton University Press, 1962), p. 130.

12. James H. Cone, *God of the Oppressed* (New York: Seabury Press, 1975), pp. 111–112.

13. See Hans W. Frei, *The Identity of Jesus Christ* (Philadelphia: Fortress Press, 1975), and *The Eclipse of Biblical Narrative* (New Haven, Conn.: Yale University Press, 1974). See also George A. Lindbeck, *The Nature of Doctrine* (Philadelphia: Westminster Press, 1984), especially chapter 6.

14. Kelsey uses this term in describing Barth's interpretation of scripture; see *The Uses of Scripture in Recent Theology*, p. 43.

15. John H. Leith, *Assembly at Westminster* (Richmond: John Knox Press, 1973), pp. 76–77.

16. *Book of Confessions*, Presbyterian Church (U.S.A.), 6.052, 6.008, 5.002. Subsequent references are to this edition.

17. John Calvin, *Commentary on a Harmony of the Evangelists*, tr. William Pringle, vol. 1 (Grand Rapids: Wm. B. Eerdmans Publishing Co., 1956), p. 216, discussing Matthew 4:5. This passage and the one that follows are cited in William J. Bouwsma, *John Calvin: A Sixteenth-Century Portrait* (New York: Oxford University Press, 1988), pp. 121f.

18. Calvin, *Commentary on a Harmony of the Evangelists*, vol. 2, p. 89, on Luke 8:19.

19. John Calvin, *Commentary on Isaiah*, tr. William Pringle, vol. 1 (Grand Rapids: Wm. B. Eerdmans Publishing Co., 1948), p. 442.

20. *Book of Confessions*, 5.010, 6.007, 6.009.

21. See Leith, *Assembly at Westminster*, p. 77.

22. *Book of Confessions*, 9.29.

23. Ibid. 6.002, 5.003.

24. John Calvin, Preface to the Genevan editions of the Bible, *Calvini Opera* 9:825; quoted in François Wendel, *Calvin: The Origins and Development of His Religious Thought*, tr. Philip Mairet (London: William Collins Sons & Co., 1965), p. 154.

25. *Book of Confessions*, 4.021.

26. "We are not concerned here with a particular theory, but with the certainty that redemption through righteousness is *also for me*, that *also my* sins are forgiven. The decisive act of faith is recognition of the gift of God as an existential gift. Where this act of faith becomes an event in men, there come together the people of God, the people who may be witness to the world of redemption through righteousness because, by virtue of the revealed and believed Word, they were 'there' in the truest sense." Karl Barth, *Learning Jesus Christ Through the Heidelberg Catechism*, tr. Shirley C. Guthrie, Jr. (Grand Rapids: Wm. B. Eerdmans Publishing Co., 1964), p. 523.

27. *Book of Confessions*, 5.005, 6.006.

28. Ibid. 9.27, 8.11.

29. These points were made against Bultmann long ago, even by his own students. See for instance Ernst Käsemann, *New Testament Questions of Today*, tr. W. J. Montague (Philadelphia: Fortress Press, 1969), p. 52; Gerhard Ebeling, *Theology and Proclamation*, tr. John Riches (Philadelphia: Fortress Press, 1966), p. 68.

30. As Hans Frei said, there are points where the narrative "allows and even forces us to ask the question, 'Did this actually take place?'" Frei, *The Identity of Jesus Christ*, p. 140. I have discussed these matters at greater length in *Unapologetic Theology* (Louisville, Ky.: Westminster/John Knox Press, 1989), especially chapters 8 and 10.

31. John Barton has recently raised such suspicions from the standpoint of a historically oriented Old Testament scholar. See his *People of the Book? The Authority of the Bible in Christianity* (Louisville, Ky.: Westminster/John Knox Press, 1989).

32. Jeffrey Stout, who is quite sympathetic to this style of theology, worries that it can never "win a wide hearing." See Jeffrey Stout, *Ethics After Babel* (Boston: Beacon Press, 1988), p. 186.

33. "Biblical Authority and Interpretation," *Minutes of the 194th General Assembly of The United Presbyterian Church in the U.S.A., 1982,* Part I: *Journal,* pp. 316–335; see p. 328.

34. "Presbyterian Understanding and Use of Holy Scripture," *Minutes of the 123rd General Assembly of the Presbyterian Church in the U.S. [195th General Assembly of the Presbyterian Church (U.S.A.)], 1983,* Part I: *Journal,* pp. 607–617; see p. 609.

The Contemporaneity of the Brief Statement of Faith 4

George H. Kehm

"A Brief Statement of Faith: Presbyterian Church (U.S.A.)" came about as a result of the reunion, in 1983, of the two main branches of the Presbyterian Church within the United States. The Articles of Agreement of the reuniting churches called for the uniting General Assembly to appoint a committee to prepare such a statement.

There was precedent for this action in the union of the United Presbyterian Church of North America and the Presbyterian Church in the U.S.A. in 1958, which brought into being The United Presbyterian Church in the U.S.A., which was sometimes referred to as the northern Presbyterian Church. At the time of the merger, a special committee was established to develop a brief contemporary statement of faith. The Confession of 1967 was the product that finally emerged from the work of that committee. After all the debate about it was over, the reunited northern church, in ratifying it, had a strong working consensus on basic matters of theology and ethics with which to guide itself through the turbulent "revolutions" of the 1960s and 1970s.

More than any other document in that new church's *Book of Confessions*, C'67, as it came to be called, brought out the *contemporary point* of the ageless gospel of God's reconciling love in Jesus Christ. It indicated what the church should stand up for in the struggles for racial and economic justice, peace, and healthy sexual relations. Not by itself but as the leading edge of the great tradition represented by the other documents it joined, that latest confession made visible the faith wherein those living Presbyterians were united and the ethical commitments to which they were bound by that faith. That is what a new contemporary statement of faith can and should do for a church, especially a newly reunited church facing a world situation that is in many ways more confusing, more enervating, and more perilous than it was in 1967. I believe the new Brief Statement of Faith is the kind of statement the Presbyterian Church (U.S.A.) needs today precisely because it does address urgent contemporary challenges facing the church and the world, although for good reasons it does not do so as extensively as the Confession of 1967.

The Brief Statement of Faith was designed primarily for liturgical and educational use. The committee chose to develop this kind of creed in response to widespread requests from the church for a confession that could be used in worship. This desire was related to another: the desire among Presbyterians for something that would give them a clearer sense of their identity—of the basic beliefs, morality, and life-style Presbyterians affirm and aspire to. In response to this felt need, the committee developed a confession that approximated first-order religious language, the language of direct personal affirmation, rather than the second-order language of "doctrines" resulting from reflection on the first-order statements. It used quasi-narrative style, employing many metaphors to make subtle, intricate connections among all the realities talked about, in order to draw people together as a distinctive community orienting itself in a distinctive way to its past, its present world, and the promised world. Thus, while remaining faithful to the Reformed tradition and giving expression to the most important themes of the biblical message, the committee employed a style and language designed to evoke a sense of corporate identity among today's Presbyterians. That is one mark of the contemporaneity of the statement.

The need to recover a stronger sense of identity is a reflection of the cultural and theological pluralism in the Presbyterian Church today. The "problem of pluralism" is relatively new in the church. When the Confession of 1967 was written, there were only two major theological positions vying with each other: one that could be called "neo-orthodox" and another that could be called "evangelical." Old-style "liberal" theologians and "orthodox" Calvinists were only marginal voices in the Presbyterian Church's ministry at that time. The Confession of 1967 reflects the neo-orthodox view, tempered by evangelical concerns at some points. While some Presbyterians never fully accepted it, the Confession of 1967 remains a testimony to a remarkable *theological* consensus throughout the church at that time. Such a consensus cannot be said to exist today, however. Today there is a much greater variety of theologies to be found in the church, including liberation theologies of different sorts, reflecting different racial ethnic backgrounds and social situations; feminist theologies; process theology; postmodern theologies; and more. Dialogue among these kinds of theology is only beginning to develop. Consensus among them at the level of theological or doctrinal formulation has not yet been reached and is probably unattainable at this time. That is what the committee concluded, which is one of the reasons it did not attempt an elaborate theological construction such as the Confession of 1967. The committee rightly saw that what could be done and what needed to be done (if the theological diversity in the church were to be kept from hardening into entrenched factionalism) was to lift up the basic, common faith of these diverse Presbyterian Christians. The committee's own diverse membership, as well as its careful listening to individuals and groups in the church across the country during the years of its work, put it in a position to express that basic faith. Of course, only the church's ratification of the Brief Statement and inclusion of it in the *Book of Confessions* will tell whether the committee succeeded. If that happens, it will be an important contribution to the church's quest for its identity today.

There is another aspect of the church's quest for identity that the Brief Statement also tried to address. This one has to do with the problem of individualism. One of the most troubling aspects of American life is the emergence of a kind of individualism that disconnects self-fulfillment from any kind of social good. People are preoccupied with improving themselves, attaining their true potential, realizing their authentic selfhood, and so on. Popular psychology magazines and therapy groups of all sorts explain how to do this. People having trouble with one or another aspect of their pursuit of self can go to depression seminars, Weight Watchers, assertiveness-training classes, psychiatrists, counselors, or twelve-step groups. There is an enormous amount of concentration on one's emotional life, fueled by a desire to feel good about oneself. Having good relations with others is important for one's self-esteem, as is also success at one's work. At the same time the risk of failure in these areas leads many to seek a kind of fulfillment that is independent of social relations and work. Even those who are successful in work and in social relationships—at least for a time—often invest in them, not because of a sense of obligation to do good for another or to contribute to the social good, but to find the satisfactions they want for themselves. The ego becomes a kind of broker trying to satisfy its needs (and they are legion, inflated by consumerist society) as much as it can by manipulating the persons and money-making means in one's society.

Old-style "utilitarian individualism" (Robert Bellah)[1] emphasized self-reliance and hard work, but the point was not simply self-making. It aimed at producing a good product, something that would be of value to others and would benefit society as a whole. That was the ideal, and those who ruthlessly pursued wealth and power at the expense of others were regarded as inhuman, not as role models. Today, that ideal has diminished. One is content to pursue one's own individual well-being, scaled to whatever one's means allow. Loyalty to communal values or to the obligations of a religious tradition, if they are in the picture at all, rank far below those that have to do with one's own happiness, financial security, and personal freedom to pursue one's own "experimental life."[2]

The Brief Statement of Faith attempts to combat this kind of socially irresponsible individualism by affirming that human life is essentially "life in community."[3] What the Brief Statement says is that God "makes everyone, male and female, of every race and people, equally in God's image *to live as one community*" (lines 27–29, emphasis mine). From their biological beginning and childhood socialization, where it is most obvious, to the end of their maturing as adults, human beings are shaped by their relationships with other selves (and with God and nature too). Their personal fulfillment depends on their coming into "right" relationships with others, near and far, kin and strangers (and with God and nature too). From the standpoint of the Christian faith, right relationships mean essentially relationships that embody love of God and of all that God loves—other human beings along with all God's creatures. That is why, when the Brief Statement describes sin, it has to refer to violations of the total network of relations in which the self exists: relations with

God, neighbor, and nature, as well as with itself. That is also why, in describing the Holy Spirit's work of liberating individuals from bondage to sin, it speaks of this as setting them free to love God and neighbor and of binding them together in a community, the church of Jesus Christ. In that community, they are put back on track toward the fulfillment God intended for them as part of the fulfillment of the purpose of the whole creation, so that they are called to include the good of the whole human community and of all God's creatures in their vision of their own personal fulfillment. The reinvestment of their ultimate loyalty and the reshaping of their loves required for this cannot come about in any kind of privatized relationship with God but only through the character-shaping influences of a community in which the "Christomorphic" love of the one true Creator and Redeemer of the world is taught, celebrated, and embodied over and over again in all the various interactions among its individual members. Only such a community can be an empowering sign of the justice, freedom, and peace of God's kingdom, by which the whole creation is transformed in the direction of the ultimate "new heaven and new earth" for which we pray (line 63).

Those are some of the basic thrusts the Brief Statement makes against socially irresponsible individualism and privatized, self-serving religion. It does so not by naming the enemy or attacking it directly. It does so by affirming a socially responsible individualism:[4] a vision of self-fulfillment in and through a community that promotes maximizing individual gifts and abilities in ways that make for the good of the whole. And the point of this community is not to offer an enclave of private consolations in the face of an incorrigibly evil world but to provide a base for world-transforming action to universalize loyalty to God and the love that does justice and brings peace among all God's creatures. That is the positive alternative the Brief Statement poses to the rampant individualism and divisive pluralism that are threatening social cohesiveness and the purposes of both church and civil society.

There is another urgent issue for our time that is addressed by the Brief Statement, the so-called ecological crisis that has suddenly become a top priority among governments around the world. Symptoms of environmental degradation had already appeared in the 1960s, and the Confession of 1967 did give brief notice to this in its concluding section (*Book of Confessions*, 9.53). However, it was more concerned with the problems of weapons of mass destruction and nuclear war than it was with environmental stewardship. One can understand the reason for giving priority to the condemnation of such weapons and to the pursuit of world peace at that time. The quest for peace and the elimination of the threat of nuclear weapons must continue without abatement even though political relations between the Soviet Union and the United States and other NATO countries have become much more cordial and cooperative. A genuine determination to maintain peace and to work together to resolve problems seems to be present on both sides of the Iron Curtain. At the same time, the global environmental crisis has become so ominous that nations can no longer put it off for future attention. The Brief Statement anticipated *Time* magazine's "Planet of the Year" issue when it described one of the forms of sin as "threatening death to the planet entrusted to our care." Death, of course, was not meant literally in this context, as if either nuclear war or environmental pollution threatened to end all forms of life on earth. It did mean devastation of the earth's ecosystems and destruction of life forms, human and nonhuman, on such a scale that civilized societies as we know them would cease to exist.

That one line, along with the lines that affirm the goodness of creation (line 26) and God's purpose "to redeem creation" (line 36), reinforced by line 63, the reference to "God's new heaven and new earth," provides a basic theological platform for the commitment to environmental stewardship the church will have to make in the 1990s and into the next century. One could wish that more had been said on this subject. But one can be grateful that this note was struck and struck strongly.

The words "entrusted to our care" suggest a renunciation of the popular idea that the Bible authorizes human beings to have "dominion" over the earth, conquering hostile nature and taking from it whatever human beings want to enhance their survival and to satisfy their desire for delectables and comforts of every sort. We have learned very late that the plundering of the earth's resources by modern industrial societies has resulted in such environmental degradation (as well as depletion of nonrenewable resources) that millions of human lives are at risk in the industrialized countries as well as in the developing nations. Mere enlightened self-interest is enough these days to convince people that a more careful stewardship of the earth and its resources is required. It is difficult for a secular ethic of enlightened self-interest to rise above the kind of chauvinistic anthropocentrism that still sees nonhuman creatures and the earth itself as so much grist for the human mill, things of no intrinsic value and thus simply "stuff" to be transformed into things human beings find useful. Reaction against such human arrogance often takes the form of a biocentric view of the world, which sees all life forms as interdependent members of the biotic community, each having as much right as any other to exist in an intact natural habitat. Such a view is difficult to maintain in the face of the enormously greater impact upon the earth's environment and its species human beings have made in comparison to other species. That is one reason why the human species bears such a great burden of responsibility for the care of the earth, the maintenance of its ability to renew itself and to sustain human and other life on into the future.

From a Christian perspective, the fact that God has created the earth and its species gives them intrinsic value: it gives them the right to exist and to be appreciated, used, and protected so that they may continue to exist and flourish. Human beings were given the honor of being caretakers or trustees of God to cultivate and preserve the earth's vitality (Gen. 2:15). The mandate to have "dominion" over the animal kingdom (Gen. 1:26, 28) seems to have meant the right to domesticate certain animals and probably also to protect oneself against dangerous ones. Permission to kill animals for food was not part of the original mandate of God to human beings as expressed in Genesis 1 and 2 but was a kind of merciful concession on the part of God to human beings after human evil had brought enmity into relations with animals (Gen. 9:2–3). There are many obscurities surrounding these ancient traditions, but some things stand out very clearly. The earth belongs to God, and God continues to act to preserve and redeem the earth. Human beings are privileged to participate with God in this, and so reflect God's "rule." From a Christian standpoint, the model of God's rule disclosed in Jesus Christ, the "servant Lord," has to be the model for the proper human stewardship of the earth. This model demands that the well-being of God's good earth and its good creatures be placed ahead of any imagined benefit for humankind only. Human ingenuity may have to work harder to find environmentally gentler ways of feeding, sheltering, and providing satisfying jobs and cultural activities for people. Ways will have to be found to make the technology and work needed for such gentler ways sufficiently profitable and satisfying to supplant current harsh methods of agriculture and production. That is, we will need methods that are less consumptive of nonrenewable resources of energy and material, that do less damage to the soil and ecosystems of the earth, and that drastically reduce dangerous chemical and thermal pollution.

The Brief Statement's seemingly bland lines about the life-style to which Christians are called take on challenging, pointed meaning if they are connected with the demand for stewardship of the earth. To serve Christ in our daily tasks comes to mean, for starters, changing our wasteful, polluting life-styles (the way we shop, the food we eat, the clothes we wear, how we decorate and heat our houses, what we do with our garbage, the means of transportation we use). It also includes the decisions we make about the kinds of education and skills we pursue and the kinds of jobs we accept. To claim all of life for Christ includes participation in God's ongoing work to heal and redeem the creation. It will take the best scientific thought and technological ingenuity to accomplish this, as well as the best social and ethical wisdom. Ecologists and engineers; economists, corporate leaders, and politicians; farmers and industrial workers; theologians and ethicists; doctors and lawyers—literally every kind of builder of the human community—will have to collaborate to bring about the kinds of sustainable and sufficient systems of agriculture and production, and of equitable and humane political and economic systems, that are appropriate for the various nations of the world.

"Eco-justice" is the name for the ideal of a world in which the members of each society participate in bringing about a sustainable use of the earth's resources that is sufficient for the legitimate human needs of its people. It combines the environmentalist's desire for a flourishing earth with the social activist's concern for peace and justice. In truth, there is an intrinsic connection between peace and justice issues and the need to protect the delicate balances of nature and its diverse species. Jack L. Stotts reminds us that, according to scriptural tradition, shalom "is a particular environmental state . . . where the claims and needs of all are satisfied; where there is a relationship of communion between and among God and humanity and nature; where there is a balancing of all claims and needs."[5] The eco-justice vision of shalom provides a platform that can enlist the most diverse groups and individuals in a common mission in which each has something important to contribute. If the church responds strongly to this challenge, it might even become attractive again to the disaffected younger generation, which is, by virtue of its preoccupation with health and fitness, predisposed to becoming involved in the protection of the environment. The Brief Statement shows its timeliness once more in that it reminds the church that "earthkeeping" is every Christian's calling. If we truly expect a new, transfigured heaven and *earth*, we need to take up that calling with utmost urgency—while we have time. The most threatening environmental problems will either be solved in the next twenty years or it will be too late to solve them at all.

Notes

1. Robert N. Bellah et al., *Habits of the Heart* (New York: Harper & Row, Perennial Library, 1986), pp. 32–33, 336.
2. Philip Rieff, *The Triumph of the Therapeutic* (New York: Harper & Row, 1966), p. 26.
3. The words are from "Economic Justice for All," Pastoral Letter on Catholic Social Teaching and the U.S. Economy, par. 63 (Washington, D.C.: National Conference of Catholic Bishops, 1986), p. 33.
4. Bellah et al., *Habits of the Heart*, p. 155.
5. Jack L. Stotts, *Church and Society*, November-December 1984, 65.

Confessions in the Life of the Contemporary Church 5

James D. Brown

Three years after the Confession of 1967 was adopted, one of the members of the drafting committee wrote a summary of reactions to a questionnaire addressed to pastors, educators, and others throughout the United Presbyterian Church. The Rev. Kenneth Reeves had been one of the few pastors involved in the drafting process, and he had a keen interest in finding out what impact the Confession was having across the church, including the congregation he served, St. Peter's by the Sea Presbyterian Church in Rancho Palos Verdes, California.

Reeves was using the Confession extensively at St. Peter's, and in his *Short Review of the First Three Years of the Confession of 1967* he gives high marks to its significance in a congregation that had been founded a few years earlier in 1959.

> The Confession is no strange document to most officers and members. The proof of influence and shaping could be found in St. Peter's capacity to be a community of contemporary believers and disciples. The splits of some churches over cur-

> rent church emphases have never developed. The officers are relaxed, but not to the point of inaction over issues. Young couples come from a great distance to be in a church as some say which is all fresh and new in heart, mind, and spirit. The evangelical power of the Confession becomes apparent in membership classes and in personal conversation. Heart and voice are liberated to speak up about the gospel in words and phrases that attract the attention of youth and adults whose heads and actions are turned to technology and research. At St. Peter's the active use of the Confession appears to make it possible for the congregation both to attract and to hold a diverse group of people in background and expectation.[1]

Reeves had a deep investment in the Confession, and his analysis is understandably that of a true believer. At the same time, from my vantage point as the current pastor of St. Peter's by the Sea, I can attest to the continuing validity of his observation that St. Peter's is in many ways a "Confession of 1967 congregation." Members who were part of those formative years developed a common language with which to do theology and make ethical choices, and while the Confession may not have "taken" as thoroughly as Reeves wanted to believe, it was a key factor in the development of this one congregation's desire to be an agent of reconciliation in a broken world.

In thinking about the possible utility of "A Brief Statement of Faith: Presbyterian Church (U.S.A.)" in the life of congregations such as St. Peter's, I find myself juxtaposing the above affirmation with the quite dissimilar reply of one of Reeves's respondents who brushed off the entire *Book of Confessions* by saying it caused "not one ripple" in his congregation, in large measure because "we have to grab our theology very quickly" due to the many "preeminently practical problems [such] as keeping the people coming to church, financing, etc."[2]

This "theology on the run" approach exemplifies how difficult it has become to maintain a distinctively Reformed denomination in our present situation. Visit any ten Presbyterian churches and you may well discover four or five different hymnals in use, liturgies for the Lord's Supper ranging from the *Book of Common Worship* to extemporaneous prayers, and baptismal formulae including the classical language about Father, Son, and Holy Spirit as well as versions that seek to capture the mysteries of the Trinity in gender-inclusive ways or in which the ineffable nature of God's being is paramount.

Such an excursion through a cross-section of Presbyterian congregations is especially eye-opening when we come to the matter of confessions of faith. While the Confession of 1967 is still in use in some congregations, especially those with United Presbyterian roots, for the most part it is no longer functioning in our worship life as a "centering" document. Its essay-like quality makes it hard for congregations to say in unison, and its repeated call for *men* to be reconciled to God gives it the feel of a document far older than its years.

Not to be overlooked is the fact that the Confession of 1967 was made available to congregations as part of a "book" of ten confessions, and in a very real sense this was perceived as an invitation to move beyond a standard creed for worship such as the Apostles' or Nicene or portions of the Westminster Confession. On any given Sunday a typical Presbyterian congregation may now be using material from any one of the creeds in our *Book of Confessions* or a portion of the Declaration of Faith which in 1976 the General Assembly of the Presbyterian Church in the United States commended for study and use in worship even though its presbyteries had not officially adopted it. Contemporary creeds from other denominations are also very much in use, and in the midst of this increasing diversity, I have heard of a few Presbyterian congregations adopting the stance of "no creed but the Bible." Is it any wonder that so many Presbyterians are asking for a clear statement of our distinctiveness in today's church and world?

Those of us on the committee that drafted the Brief Statement of Faith became increasingly aware that our task was to write a brief, doxological statement of the Reformed faith that could serve to unify and center the members of our congregations through regular use in worship, new member classes, and educational forums. In what follows I will highlight three key areas where we have sought to clarify who we are as Presbyterian Christians: language about God, the relationship between sin and redemption, and the radical inclusivity to which we are called. In all of this I am writing from my perspective as the pastor of a congregation formed at the time the Confession of 1967 was adopted and which is now seeking to discern the Spirit's guidance for the next chapter in its life.

Language About God

Presbyterians clearly do not stand on common ground when it comes to language about God. Each time we sing the Gloria and hear someone next to us using language different from our own, we are reminded that confessing our faith with one voice is not a simple task in today's world.

Some recent dialogue in *Monday Morning*, a weekly publication for Presbyterian pastors, serves to highlight the challenge we face in finding mutually satisfactory language about God. One pastor writes: "Am I the only one in the Presbyterian Church (U.S.A.) upset by what seems to be an idolatrous regard for the trinitarian baptismal formula 'Father, Son, and Holy Spirit' in the new proposed *Directory for Worship*? . . . There are women (and men) in my congregation for whom insisting on baptism in the name of 'the Father' would be enough to prevent them from joining the Christian community. . . . I for one have no intention of following this mandate."[3] Several respondents were quick to express shock and dismay, with one writer saying that "to steal our sacramental language, the historic revelation of the Gospels, and the words we believe are instituted by Christ, is to steal from us that which we hold most dear."[4]

The impetus behind this debate is the conviction of an increasing number of people that our words for God are so tangled in patriarchal imagery that we should restrict ourselves to language that points to the "wholly other" aspect of God's eternal being, such as the "I AM WHO I AM" of Exodus 3:14. But as Mary Collins says so well, "The unknowability of God is not the premise of the liturgical assembly. The premise of the liturgy is that God's self-disclosure is occasion for celebration, for praise and thanks and intercession. Rightly or wrongly people who assemble for liturgy assume the divine presence and anticipate communion with the living God who continues to speak a word of invitation."[5]

A tradition that has close to its heart a prayer which begins "Our Father . . ." cannot simply ignore a metaphor for God that is found 187 times in the Gospels. The Brief Statement (line 25) therefore picks up Jesus' own language where in the agony of Gethsemane he prays, "Abba, Father" (Mark 14:36). There is much scholarly debate about whether "Abba" is simply a common Aramaic word for father, or one that evokes the moving intimacy of a child's earliest recognition of a loving parent. The fact that the Aramaic word is left untranslated here and in Romans 8:15 and Galatians 4:6 leads many to conclude that in the early church the word "Abba" opened up new and saving insight into the nature of God. Gail Ramshaw-Schmidt puts it like this: "Jesus' God is Abba, the loving parent, the gracious papa, the nurturing mother, the one who hears the cry of the servant [Jesus], who receives the servant in human chaos and by being there transfigures the chaos of the cross into the meaning we call resurrection. This is truly astonishing, not only that there is a God in our chaos but that God is Abba."[6]

The inclusion of the word "Abba" in the text of the Brief Statement adds an element of creative dissonance, an untranslatable invitation into bonds of intimacy with the God who comes close to us in Jesus Christ. The parable of the prodigal son, as much as any New Testament passage, gives substance to the meaning of "Abba," for there the father astonishes Jesus' listeners by, in the words of Kenneth Bailey, running to meet his son *as a mother might do.*[7] Abba, then, is a metaphor that entices us into transcending our macho stereotypes and sharing the amazement of Jesus' listeners who had the ears to hear and the faith to imagine a God who is "like a mother who cannot forget her nursing child, like a father who runs to welcome the prodigal home" (lines 41–42).

Beginning with the language of Jesus for God is just that: a beginning. This unites us with those who have come before us and with sister churches with whom we stand in the present moment. But we should never forget that it is the Holy Spirit who gives our words meaning, and the Holy Spirit is making all things new, including our perceptions of the living God. Therefore, as services of worship are prepared, sacraments administered, and sermons preached, we need to be about the joyful task of seeking complementary images for a God who cannot be contained by any one metaphor. In so doing, Presbyterians can fulfill what I believe to be a significant part of our unique calling in a world in dire need of practicing the presence of a God in whose image both male and female are fashioned.

Sin and Redemption

The Brief Statement differs from past confessions which have been used extensively in worship, such as the Apostles' Creed and the Nicene Creed, in the manner in which the confessing community is asked to declare its deep and pervasive complicity in rebellion against God. Worshipers sometimes find it unsettling to be mixing words of affirmation with expressions of personal sinfulness, but to my way of thinking, this promises to be one of the Brief Statement's most significant contributions at the local church level.

Recently a pastor from the Reformed Church in Czechoslovakia visited the congregation I serve, and in a private conversation he expressed his surprise and dismay that the most frequent question he heard parishioners ask after worship was, "Did you enjoy the service?" As he pressed his point that churchgoers in the United States seem to have an overriding need to be entertained in worship, I found myself thinking about a lecture I had heard over twenty years ago. The psychoanalyst Philip Rieff predicted that Calvinism's stress on judgment and redemption would gradually give way to what he called "the triumph of the therapeutic," that is, to personal growth through private therapy and an appreciation of the arts.[8] Our Czech visitor sensed that the sober recognition of human fallenness and our need for redemption which is at the core of our Genevan heritage had been dramatically diluted by a desire for pleasure and personal fulfillment. In point of fact, there are a fair number of Presbyterian congregations which have removed prayers of confession from worship because they are a "downer" and make people feel discouraged.

Needless to say, there has been some criticism about the negative overtones created by cataloging our sins in the course of a confession of faith. Yet when I presented the Brief Statement to a group of high school and college students, they expressed relief that their elders in the faith had dared to face up to the pervasive rebellion that does indeed threaten the planet and its inhabitants. For them, to acknowledge the ecological crisis, the nuclear threat, and the despair that leads so many of their contemporaries to numb themselves with alcohol and drugs, is an essential step toward ethical and spiritual liberation. They said that all too often the church participates in an avoidance of reality and thus colludes in their impoverishment when it comes to developing the kinds of convictions and beliefs that will enable them to participate in God's inbreaking reign of justice and mercy.

In this account it is important to note that at the 1989 General Assembly in Philadelphia, the one word in the Brief Statement that received the most attention was "judgment," which is found in the line which concludes the section on rebellion against God: "We deserve God's judgment" (line 35). The issue boiled down to a choice between the word "condemnation," which was used in an earlier draft, and "judgment"; and the General Assembly ultimately voted 311 to 257 to recommend a return to the language, "We deserve God's condemnation."

From the vantage point of the pastorate, the debate is anything but trivial. As we confess our awful complicity in the degradations of our age, we are acknowledging before God that we are redeemed by grace alone. When Isaiah came face to face with the living God, his immediate reaction was, "Woe is me! For I am lost; for I am a man of unclean lips, and I dwell in the midst of a people of unclean lips" (Isa. 6:5). We, too, experience a sense of lostness as human beings when we confront our sinfulness. For some, the word "condemnation" sends a message that it is too late, that we are beyond hope. For others, "judgment" is a soft word which suggests that we are not so bad after all.

As I have said, this is not an insignificant debate, for at stake is the passage between guilt and deliverance, the miraculous movement from sin to redemption. In a world always in danger of losing its nerve, how do we confess our need for unmerited grace while at the same time recognizing the fragile psyches and spirits of the recovering alcoholics and single parents and disillusioned children who struggle to hang on to enough self-worth to get them through another day and another week?

At the heart of our faith is the conviction that while we are always judged by God's righteousness, we are never finally condemned, because in Jesus Christ we have come to know God as both just *and* merciful. The efficacy of the Brief Statement at this point hinges on a reality that cannot be adequately captured in human language. When we say we deserve God's judgment or condemnation, we do so in the remembered expectation that we will hear in the inner recesses of our hearts and souls what Isaiah heard: "Your guilt is taken away, and your sin forgiven" (Isa. 6:7). Only if this Word is heard will the next line make any sense to the beleaguered and precious human beings who sit in the pews and chancels of our congregations: "Yet God rules with justice and mercy to redeem creation" (line 36).

Radical Inclusivity

The final aspect of the Brief Statement I want to highlight from my perspective as a local church pastor is the one which asserts that the Holy Spirit "calls women and men to all ministries of the church" (line 53). My belief is that the elevation of this aspect of our denomination's life to confessional status will have a healing and liberating impact every time the Brief Statement is used.

Until now most of the debates about the ordination of women have been carried out along the lines of polity. This has led to the dilemma that whereas our political will has been established, we still have a long way to go in overcoming the centuries-old taboos against female leadership in the church. Although few of our members give much credence to the admonition of the Second Helvetic Confession that women cannot officiate at baptisms, there still is the inability on the part of many—both male and female—to celebrate the way in which the Spirit is at long last liberating the church from its centuries-old patriarchal straitjacket. This is made painfully evident when women elders cannot bring themselves to serve communion because they feel they are treading on forbidden ground, or when male pastors say they cannot in good conscience participate in the ordination of women elders.

Just before the meeting of the General Assembly in Philadelphia in June of 1989, the World Council of Churches sponsored a World Conference on Mission and Evangelism in San Antonio, Texas. The position taken there on the ordination of women by participants from Orthodox Churches underscores the deep roots of the tradition of male-only leadership.

Bishop Antonius Markos of Egypt spoke on behalf of the Orthodox participants in San Antonio when he said: "The confession of the holy name of the Father, the divinity of the Son, and existence of the Holy Spirit as an hypostasis [person] and their unity in the divine essence of God is the fundamental presupposition of the participation of the Orthodox Churches in the World Council of Churches." Bishop Markos then drew from this premise the assertion that the ordination of women to the priesthood is "not, for us, subject to debate, since it is contrary to the Christology, ecclesiology, tradition, and practice" of the church throughout the ages.[9]

Of deep concern to Presbyterians is how we are to navigate the ecumenical seas with companions holding such divergent theologies. Not to be overlooked is the lingering male "iconography" of our own traditions as we seek to build a model of ministry where all—ordained and nonordained, male and female—are one in Christ Jesus. Raising our commitment to radical inclusivity to confessional status is one of the ways we stake out our integrity as a denomination and invite our members to celebrate the biblical vision we have embraced. By so doing we also make a witness in the ecumenical world to the claim we believe Christ is making on all members of his body. And we do this with real humility during a time when a number of our own congregations continue to deny leadership roles to women and in some cases are leaving our denomination over this issue.

A heartening outcome of the furor set off by Bishop Markos's remarks in San Antonio and a harbinger of things to come, I believe, was his concession that "any woman ordained by her own church, if her church accepts her, we will give all respect."[10] Every time a congregation affirms that the Spirit "calls women and men to all ministries of the church," the ongoing sanctification of God's people is facilitated. Becoming more respectful of one another's gifts, especially the gifts of those who have been marginalized for so long, is surely one of the special blessings of God in our time.

Perhaps one of the most important things a confession can do is expose for all to see those beliefs and causes which have our deepest respect. By declaring our commitment to overcoming the taboos which belittle and abuse others, we show that we really do believe that all are made equally in God's image—male and female, of every race and people.

Conclusion

During the course of serving on the committee writing the Brief Statement of Faith, I read somewhere that the "magic" comes not so much in reading something, but in the rereading. I think this is especially true regarding our character formation as Christians and congregations, and I think Presbyterians desperately need the oft-repeated language of a common testimony at this moment in our history.

We are now a national denomination, but it is important to remember that our reunion has come at a time of increasing "decoupling" from denominational loyalties. Of the new members received each year by St. Peter's by the Sea, roughly half have had no prior ties to the Reformed tradition. If our denomination is to survive as more than a loose-knit confederation of increasingly regionalized and independent congregations, we will have to agree on some basic building blocks that bear repeating. My experience is that men and women are attracted to our Presbyterian way of practicing the faith when we give them a biblically grounded alternative to the dominant religion in our society: a narcissistic secularism that has as its unwritten creed the avoidance of honesty and self-knowledge. The study and recitation of the creeds of the faith can be a powerful antidote and a real source of hope.

Karl Barth's answer to a questioner who asked him to summarize a life's work that filled thousands of pages in his *Church Dogmatics* and other books was disarmingly simple: "Jesus loves me, this I know, for the Bible tells me so." With such a reply he confirmed something rooted in our own experience. We learn our faith in communities where songs are sung and litanies recited and faith is declared—and all of these acts are repeated again and again. Presbyterians need to take the risk of singing from a common hymnal and using services for the Lord's Day that contain prayers and liturgies for the sacraments which connect us north and south, east and west. And we need to use our confessional heritage, with the Brief Statement as one starting point, in preaching and adult study, in communicants' and new member classes, and in the training of elders and deacons. Otherwise our Reformed distinctives may become things for historians to study, not marks of a living tradition.

A number of years ago I was talking with a Baptist friend about the differences between his congregation and mine when it came to creeds. When I said that I saw his theological heritage as basically one of "no creed but the Bible," he said that this was really not the case. In fact, he pointed out that many Baptist churches post in their narthexes statements containing a mixture of such things as belief in scriptural inerrancy and a prohibition against drinking. In the case of his own congregation, he said that the last time the narthex was painted their statement of beliefs was taken down and never put back up, in part because it no longer reflected the character of his congregation as well as it had twenty or thirty years before. He then went on to say that he wished Baptists had developed something like our *Book of Confessions*, for he felt this gave us a means for developing a disciplined, evolutionary way of staying grounded in our past while at the same time engaging the emerging issues facing the church and world.

For my friend's assessment to be valid, Presbyterians in every generation need a window into their confessional heritage, something to fill the place held by the Shorter Catechism in days gone by. This cannot come without broad biblical, theological, and historical study carried on in every congregation. But in an age of much confusion, we cannot ignore the need for bedrock, narrowed-down vocabulary with which to talk about such things as our "chief end," our destiny in life and in death as followers of Jesus Christ.

The Brief Statement of Faith is being offered as one such window. My fervent hope is that, in congregations such as St. Peter's by the Sea, it will be used by the Holy Spirit to help us regain a powerful sense of who we are meant to be as Presbyterian Christians, and to energize us for our liberating work within the household of God and the world God loves so much.

Notes

1. *A Short Review of the First Three Years of the Confession of 1967*, by Kenneth E. Reeves, 1970, p. 6. Copies of this paper are available from St. Peter's by the Sea Presbyterian Church, Rancho Palos Verdes, CA 90274.
2. Ibid., pp. 1–2.
3. Jeffrey K. Krehbiel, "Upset by the *Directory for Worship*," *Monday Morning*, April 17, 1989, 17–18.

4. Chet Okopski, "Sacramental Language," *Monday Morning*, June 1989, 9.

5. Mary Collins, "Naming God in Public Prayer," *Worship* 59/4 (July 1985), 293.

6. Gail Ramshaw-Schmidt, "Naming the Trinity: Orthodoxy and Inclusivity," *Worship* 60/6 (November 1986), 496.

7. Kenneth E. Bailey, "Our Father: Did Jesus Define His Term?" *The Presbyterian Outlook*, 171/24 (June 19, 1989), 6–7.

8. Philip Rieff's book, *The Triumph of the Therapeutic* (Harper & Row, 1966), continues to offer helpful insights into the search for individualistic self-fulfillment that is so pervasive in today's world.

9. *Ecumenical Press Service*, 56/20, June 16–30, 1989 (89.06.21) (World Council of Churches, Geneva).

10. Ibid.

Inclusive Language and the Brief Statement of Faith: Widening the Margins in Our Common Confession 6

Clarice J. Martin

In his discussion of the character of the newly reunited Presbyterian Church, Jack Rogers describes the Presbyterian Church (U.S.A.) as a denomination that seeks continually to define and affirm its faith as a confessing Reformed church. The confessions, outlining what is essential for us to believe and act upon as a believing community, pose helpful limits about what we believe and uniquely offer to the ecumenical mix.[1] But there is "latitude" within those limits to confess our faith anew in every generation, informed by new insights both from the Word of God and from the Reformed community:

> A word processor or personal computer has preprogrammed margins, on the left and on the right. Within these margins, we have complete freedom to write what we want, changing and experimenting at will. We can also alter these margins, making them wider or narrower. But we cannot function without some kind of margin on either side. Neither can we in our denomination live peaceably together and move forward in mission unless we know what is essential and necessary for us

and what is the area in which we have freedom of individual conscience. We need to be confessional—positively appropriating our Reformed heritage.[2]

It is the thesis of this essay that as we confess our faith in this period of the denomination's life and history, we must "widen the margins" of the language and imagery that we use for God. This means that we must consciously incorporate the whole range of imagery and metaphor for God available to us in scripture, including feminine and masculine imagery, and the imagery for God that is not gender-related. The impetus for this conscious "readjustment" of the margins or limits of our theological discourse about God is prompted not only by major societal shifts toward more inclusive language usage for females and males in the public and private spheres.[3] More important, the use of inclusive language is rooted in the biblical witness itself. The church is called to be faithful to all of scripture used to talk to God and about God.[4] Only then can our creeds, prayers, hymns, educational curricula, and other forms of communicative discourse in our corporate life represent the richness and wealth mirrored in scripture itself.

Language and Androcentric Bias

Feminist critiques of patriarchy (a society characterized by the "manifestation and institutionalization of male dominance over women and children in the family and the extension of male dominance over women in society in general"[5]) have underscored and documented the pervasiveness of male dominance in both society and language. Words, in particular, functioning as meaning carriers, help to generate and shape ideologies and attitudes which, in turn, shape and influence the psychosocial world of women, men, and children alike. The premise that "men" and "maleness" represent normative humanity, and that male domination in public and sacred space is ideologically, structurally, and theologically acceptable and desirable has permeated the pre- and post-Enlightenment Western world for centuries. It has undergirded an androcentric (male-centered) worldview. Since women have been largely excluded from the production of cultural forms and legitimated language, they have been unable either to give weight to their own symbolic meanings or to pass on traditions of women's interpretations and meanings of the world.[6]

Patriarchal domination and androcentric bias have contributed to a world that has severely limited women's opportunities to pursue occupations and vocations where they can significantly shape and influence ontological and epistemological theory. Dale Spender has noted that while women have philosophized, made speeches, written poetry, and held theories about language and the world, "they have not had the same opportunity to influence the language, to introduce new meanings where they will be taken up, to define the objects or events of the world. . . . The meanings which they have generated and which have diverged from those of men have not always gained access to the public arena, have not always been central to the culture."[7] Consequently, determinations of what is "significant" or "important" in our symbolic universe have usually been made by males. As Mary Daly has observed, it is males who have named the world, and "it is probably inevitable that those who perform naming should do so from their own point of view, taking themselves as the center, the reference point, and naming all else in relation to themselves."[8]

The tendency toward androcentric bias in general societal discourse and epistemological paradigms is well documented. In the academic arena, for example, females have been largely omitted from scholarship as researchers, subjects of research, and as definers of knowledge—in short, from historical significance.[9] Research methodologies assume the superiority of maleness and males as normative subjects in research projects.[10] In fact, traditional education research focuses almost exclusively on male activities.[11]

Edwin Ardener has shown that there is a tendency for male anthropologists to consult only males within other cultural contexts while engaged in anthropological research on the social and ideological composition of those cultures.[12] Images of women in literary works often reflect the standards of femininity defined in accordance with men's views of appropriate biologically and socially determined roles.[13] Marlene Mackie and others have shown that in sociological research male sociologists have tended to focus their research on settings where males predominate, including the political and legal system, while at the same time leaving virtually untouched such topics as women's social behavior (unless it impinged on men's lives), motherhood, women's domestic labor, women's medicine, widowhood, and women's roles in cultural production. The underlying premise seems to be that no one really cares to read studies about women, their dilemmas, their problems, and their attempts at solutions.[14]

Feminists in educational psychology have shown that a male perspective prevails in the conceptualization and analysis of such topics as personality, interpersonal interaction, learning theory, social roles, intelligence, and achievement.[15] In response to feminist critiques of education research methodologies and curricula, females were added to traditional paradigms as an intended corrective to the problem of male bias. The problem with this "add women and stir" method is, of course, that it assumes that the theories, paradigms, and their underlying assumptions about human nature are legitimate.[16]

In short, androcentric bias has regularly promoted the invisibility, silence, and alienation of women in a variety of disciplines. These disciplines have not affirmed women as legitimate creators and interpreters of knowledge, and they have often trivialized the "feminine," as well as women's critiques and contributions.

Androcentrism, in general, and male dominance in language, in particular, have undergone renewed scrutiny in the last three decades. In 1956 the linguist Simon Podair observed that language is more than a mere communicative device:

> Language not only expresses ideas and concepts but it may actually shape them. Often the process is completely unconscious with the individual concerned unaware of the influence of the spoken or written expressions upon . . . his thought processes. Language can thus become an instrument of both propaganda and indoctrination of a given idea.[17]

Language can function as a transmitter, symbolic system, and social leveler,[18] and it can also be used to reinforce or entrench social inequality. As Haig Bosmajian observes, the language of sexism reinforces the "superiority" of the male and "inferiority" of the female, relegating women and the feminine to subordinate status as "the second sex."[19] The predominance of the masculine pronoun "he" and the noun "man" as a generic for both women and men "blankets" or "conceals" women under a masculine identity and renders them invisible. Even grammarians have treated the masculine gender as first in order of creation and importance in the natural world and in sentence structure, in short, as "the most worthy gender."[20] This tendency toward male priority is clearly seen in a listing of the name of popular female and male storybook and dramatic characters: Jack and Jill, Hansel and Gretel, Romeo and Juliet, Antony and Cleopatra, Dick and Jane. One of the few examples of female priority in syntactical structure is Snow White and the Seven Dwarfs.[21]

If exclusive (male) language "conceals" women or depicts

them as the "less worthy gender," inclusive language seeks to include, rather than exclude, to give a full and unbiased view of female and male humanity with responsible and equitable regard for the full range of their human potential and personhood as well as their limitations. Inclusive language names and affirms female and male particularity where appropriate. Male gender-specific descriptions often require a vigilant examination of the semantic field (or context) to determine whether the term could apply to a female. Such phrases as "the best man for the job" and "men of the future," and titles such as "chairman" or "juryman" require a careful examination of context clues to determine if women or men are signified. Joan Huber alludes to the very real problems of semantic ambiguity effectuated by exclusive male nouns and pronouns: "To use 'men' to mean both 'men' and 'women and men' is an exercise in double-think."[22] Using language to foster accuracy, precision, and inclusivity in our allusions to all human persons has been increasingly recognized as indispensable in a society that is committed to promoting justice in social relationships.

Inclusive Language for God: The Dialogue Continues

> Dear God,
> Are boys better than girls? I know that you are one but try to be fair.
>
> Sylvia[23]

If the need to incorporate more inclusive epistemological and linguistic models for human persons has been gaining ascendancy in academic and other arenas, ecclesiastical communities have witnessed a proliferation of literature on this subject as well. In 1973, the United Presbyterian Church U.S.A. initiated two major studies of language for human beings and language about God which culminated in the publication of a resource document entitled *The Power of Language Among the People of God and the Language About God: "Opening the Door": A Resource Document.*[24] Inclusive-language lectionaries have become available for conregational use.[25] An ever-increasing array of articles, books, and other resource materials on the power and funcion of language in theological discourse is now available.[26]

The subject of inclusive language for God has engendered valuable (if sometimes polemical) discussions on a complex range of issues. Rogers has identified some of them: "For some, it is a conflict between radical feminist politics and traditional biblical texts. For others it is a confusion over the relationship between the Bible, various kinds of translations of the Bible, lectionary readings from the Bible, and teaching about the Bible."[27] Also relevant are questions of biblical authority and the interpretation of biblical languages (Hebrew, Greek, Aramaic) and traditions that were written in patriarchal cultures and that also betray a decisively male interest and orientation.[28]

The increased usage of inclusive language for God in ecclesiastical communities across the denominational spectrum is prompted by at least two factors. First, inclusive language usage has warrant within the Bible.[29] The Judeo-Christian message about the full humanity of all persons (Gen. 1:27; 2:4–25: both female and male are made in the image of God) means that full personhood should be expressed linguistically, for both females and males fully image God, and the experiences of women and men are appropriate and equally worthy metaphors for God's creative, saving, nurturing, and empowering activity.[30]

Among the many female images for God in the biblical revelation are references to God as one who, like a mother, conceives and nurtures children (Num. 11:12; Hos. 11:3–4), and who like a mother gives birth (Deut. 32:18). God is also like a mother bear (Hos. 13:7–8) and a mother eagle (Deut. 32:11).

Jesus compared God to the woman who added yeast to flour while baking bread and the farmer who sowed mustard seeds (Matt. 13:31–33; Luke 13:18–21). Jesus used a woman as a symbol of God in his discussion of God's activity in seeking the lost: Like a woman who persistently sweeps her house for the precious silver coin which she has lost, God seeks women and men for eternal salvation (Luke 15:8–10; cf. vs. 1–7).

It is noteworthy that wide-ranging female images for God have been retained in biblical traditions produced and transmitted in patriarchal societies where females and "the feminine" were generally perceived as both subordinate and inferior.[31] The biblical writers, recognizing that human language cannot adequately or wholly describe the God of Judaism and Christianity, employed a vast range of metaphors (implicit comparisons in which one thing is described in terms of another, and which "finds the vein of similarity in the midst of dissimilars"[32]), and images for God from human experience to portray God's transcendence and ineffability, and to affirm God's activity and relationship with human persons. "We have no other language besides metaphor with which to speak about God."[33] Metaphors, far more than "poetic ornamentation" or "rhetorical color," are powerful figures that enable us to speak about what transcends and affects us at the deepest level of our existence.[34]

The predominance of exclusive male imagery for God and humankind has, in the view of many theologians, biblical scholars, and clergy, promoted the idolatrous view of God as male—a fact suggested by little Sylvia's quote above. Male-biased language in scripture, tradition, and church makes it difficult to affirm what most Christians readily concede verbally, that God is not a human male, but that God is transcendent and beyond sexuality.

> While most theologians readily acknowledge the biblical view that sexuality is not to be attributed to God, some nevertheless insist that male images of God are not only fitting and proper but also *essential* and *irreplaceable*. . . . The pervasive and enduring male imagery for God makes difficult if not impossible an understanding of God that is beyond sexuality—hence idolatry.[35]

That the use of exclusive male language, imagery, and symbols has served as theological justification for the subordination of women in the church (as well as the larger society) is widely recognized.[36] Sexual identity rather than interest or capability is often still determinative in decisions about patterns and structures of leadership.[37] For centuries the church, with its tradition of patriarchy and women's subordination, has reinforced prevailing societal norms that relegated women to the domestic spheres and to marginal leadership roles. Women's status and identity were achieved and advanced primarily through marriage and childbearing.[38] Images of God as a powerful old man with a white beard, and the interpretation of the word "Father" to mean that God is *literally* male have promoted the imaging of God as a male.[39] Daly summarizes the consequences of such thinking succinctly: "If God is male, then the male is God":[40]

> If God in "his" heaven is a father ruling "his" people, then it is in the "nature" of things and according to divine plan and the order of the universe that society be male-dominated. Within this context a mystification of roles takes place. . . . The images and values of a given society have been projected into the realm of dogmas and "Articles of Faith," and these in turn justify the social structures which have given rise to them and which sustain their plausibility.[41]

Inclusive language usage for God not only enlarges our vocabulary and understanding of God beyond the patriarchal male-dominated model. It also constitutes in the final analysis a matter of faithfulness to the God who in scripture is revealed in a plurality of metaphors and images, and who cannot be contained in gender-defined models.

We conclude, then, that one major reason for the increased usage of inclusive language for God is the growing recognition that the Bible itself employs female and male metaphors and images for God. A second reason for encouraging inclusive language usage for God is that the *omission* of female imagery and other nonmasculine imagery for God in theological discourse often leads to the erroneous conclusion that female and other nonmasculine imagery for God is of negligible theological consequence.

David Buttrick has shown that while the interaction of language and perception is multidimensional, it is true that language can function as a grid, heightening some perceptions while screening out others. "So, though language names the world, a converse may be remarked: *what is unnamed may not be for us*."[42] The idea that the rich array of images for God in scripture "may not be for us" must be approached with caution.[43] A plurality of biblical images can constitutively and functionally enrich and enlarge our understanding of God. In fact, the language about God that is most reliable is that which employs the widest possible range of models.[44]

The importance of taking feminine as well as masculine imagery for God seriously is illustrated in a dialogue that took place between two campus ministers, Toni and Charlie, during a worship service at St. Jerome's College, University of Waterloo, Ontario. The dialogue was designed to challenge worship participants to recover feminine imagery for God in their individual and corporate life. After reciting more than twenty female images for God in the Old and New Testaments, Toni continues:

Toni: And there's more, you know. In Psalm 22:9–10, God is a female midwife.

Charlie: Maybe so. But I still say the best images of God are the strong ones. He is called "Rock," you know, and that's a pretty masculine-sounding description.

Toni: "You were unmindful of the Rock that begot you, you forgot the God who gave you birth." That's Deuteronomy 32:18. I don't know many *men* who have given birth—do you?

Charlie: Not lately anyway. But look, we're not supposed to take the idea of God giving birth *literally* are we?

Toni: Of course not. But we should take it *seriously*, because it reveals something true about the nature of God.

Charlie: You mean it tells us that God is *not* male.

Toni: More than that—it tells us that in many ways God is like a *woman*.[45]

As Toni's comments indicate, the recovery of female imagery for God in scripture can function not only as a corrective to the tendency to become reductionistic (and male-exclusive) in the language that we use for God. The task of recovering feminine and non-gender-related imagery for God (God as Light, Fire, Rock, Potter, Shield) is an invitation to engage in the constructive theological task of discovering that the whole range of biblical metaphors and imagery tells us about the nature and activity of God. Drawing upon the full range of imagery for God can attenuate the tendency to take any one set of verbal images literally, reminding us that "God is like but also unlike any verbal analogy."[46] By "widening the margins" and expanding our thinking about God beyond the boundaries of a still-powerful patriarchal conditioning, we recall that God is transcendent, beyond limitation. Inclusive language for God invites us to probe the mystery behind theological language[47] and to explore the exciting and diverse ways that God has chosen to exist in relationship to women and men.

Widening the Margins of Our Confessional Language and Church Renewal

The enigmatic brevity of creeds does not mask their profundity or their power ever to recall, broaden, and deepen the meaning of Christian faith in the lives of individual believers and the corporate community. It is true that the correct starting point for a confession is the triune God, for "it is in the light of the self-disclosure of the triune God that societal and personal structures are ultimately to be understood and transformed."[48] And yet, the language, concepts and terms of the creeds, including the language about the triune God, have always been reflective of a particular time and place. "The *Sitz im Leben* determines even the style and form of the creed."[49]

Creedal statements elucidate and interpret the Christian message in different historical and cultural circumstances, requiring a "living encounter" between the biblical revelation and persons living in particular places and times. The language and imagery used in the articles of a creed are most consequential:

> An exchange between the gospel and a new existential situation requires a new expression of the Christian message. . . . Language and its conceptual elements are embedded in a particular historical and social fabric. This means that the Christian message must be translated anew regularly if it is to be intelligent and have an impact on people's lives. Formulating a creed, therefore, obviously requires both fidelity and creativity, not only memory but imagination.[50]

In this period of our denominational life as the Presbyterian Church (U.S.A.), we are searching for ways faithfully and responsibly to enlarge our language about God. We are doing so to nurture, sustain, and empower the *whole* church in the service of a more authentic and historically faithful ecclesial koinonia. Therefore it is appropriate that the language in our creedal formulations be *more explicitly inclusive* of both female and male participation in the drama of salvation history, and that it incorporate a broader range of metaphors and images for God. If, in fact, gender reference is necessary in expressing a creed's faith at all, reference need not be limited to one gender.[51]

The Brief Statement of Faith provides a clear example of God's providential working through both female and male humanity to achieve the divine plan within human history. In lines 37–38, the Brief Statement affirms:

> Through Abraham and Sarah God chose a covenant people
> to bless all the families of the earth.

Discussions of the covenant traditions in Genesis 17 often highlight God's dealings with Abraham, rendering Sarah almost invisible. But there are more than thirty references to Sarah in the Old Testament, some of which are found in Genesis 17. "Unearthing" Sarah from the dust of patriarchal centuries[52] will show that she is more than the "biological instrument" through whom God's promise to "bless all the nations of the earth" would be fulfilled (Gen. 12:1–9; 15:1–6). Israel's origin in and continuity with Abraham *and* Sarah are emphasized in several places in scripture.[53] God changes the names of both Abraham and Sarah (Gen. 12:1–3; 17:15–16). Just as God promised to make Abraham a "father of nations" (Gen. 17:5), God promised to make Sarah a "mother of nations" (Gen. 17:16): "Kings of peoples shall come from her" (Gen. 17:16). Both Abraham and Sarah laughed at the thought of bearing children in their old age (Gen. 17:17;

18:11–12). Both Abraham and Sarah discovered that faith in God concerns the humanly impossible[54] with the miraculous blessing of the birth of their son Isaac (Gen. 21:1–7).

Of the five New Testament allusions to Sarah (Rom. 4:19; 9:9; Gal. 4:21–31; Heb. 11:11; 1 Peter 3:6), Hebrews 11:11 is especially provocative. Standing with Abraham as the female head of the lineage through which the Messiah would come, Sarah, the matriarch of faithful believers, is remembered for her faith in the God whom she considered faithful. Her faithfulness is remembered and recorded with Abraham's, for she, with Abraham and other early witnesses, "died in faith, not having received what was promised, but having seen it and greeted it from afar" (Heb. 11:13).

In his discussion of the Abraham and Sarah traditions, Ralph W. Klein reminds us that Sarah's full participation in the covenantal account in Genesis 17 "is important for both Jews and Christians today as we strive to be more inclusive in our language."[55] The journey and obedience of this patriarch and matriarch of faithful believers serve to remind us that both females and males are invited to engage in a life of trusting obedience, service, and responsibility to God.[56]

The male-female parallelism in the covenantal language of the Brief Statement of Faith is complemented by female and male imagery for God in lines 39–42:

> As heirs in Christ of the covenant,
> we know God remains faithful still,
> like a mother who cannot forget her nursing child,
> like a father who runs to welcome the prodigal home.

The similes comparing God to a mother and father in lines 41–42 provide a lucid and arresting picture of the immensity and steadfastness of God's faithfulness. In Isaiah 49:1ff., Zion's despair is depicted in graphic terms: Zion feels both despised by the nations (Isa. 49:7) and abandoned and forsaken by God (Isa. 49:14). "Zion believed that she was completely forgotten of her God."[57] The prophet uses an emphatic rhetorical question to assert God's steadfast love for Zion in Isaiah 49:15, drawing on the imagery of a mother to portray God's intimate, life-giving bond to the covenant people:

> "Can a woman forget her sucking child,
> that she should have no compassion
> on the son of her womb?"
> Even these may forget,
> yet I will not forget you.

The implication of the prophet's statement is clear: it is almost inconceivable that a woman could forget her nursing child, recently, and most intimately, a part of her own biological being. It is almost unthinkable that a mother should forget the child who is dependent on her continually night and day. But even if the tender bond of love and intimacy is broken between a mother and her nursing child, God will never forget Zion. The powerful figure of maternal love underscores God's steadfast love: "graven on the palms" of God's hands, Israel is the beloved object of Yahweh's perennial and focused concern (Isa. 49:16–26). "Yahweh's fidelity to his covenant and his promises demanded that Zion be a particular object of his saving love."[58]

Similarly, God's fidelity exceeds even what could be expected of a father: God welcomes even disobedient children. Luke 15 narrates a scene in which Pharisees and scribes murmur against Jesus for welcoming and dining with tax collectors and sinners (Luke 15:1–2). Jesus tells three parables that illustrate God's love for the outcast and desire for the recovery of the lost (the man and the lost sheep, Luke 15:3–7; the woman and the lost coin, Luke 15:8–10; the prodigal son, Luke 15:11–32).

In the parable of the prodigal son, the father shows compassion toward his repentant younger son whose bacchanalian excursion "into a far country" left him penniless and forlorn (Luke 15:11–16). The father, seeing his son returning home at yet some distance away, "ran and embraced him and kissed him" (Luke 15:20). The active verbs in verse 20 demonstrate the poignant and compelling truth that the father refuses to allow the separation of the younger son to continue.[59] Despite the depth of sinfulness of God's wayward people, God's love for God's own people never fails. God remains ever faithful to the divine covenant, compassionate, ready to forgive.

The juxtaposition of female and male parental imagery portrays the pertinacious character of God's faithfulness and illustrates the power of gender-inclusive language to provide a ray of light, through windows familiar and unfamiliar, that protracts our understanding of the nearness of love of an omnipotent God. Bernard L. Marthaler avers that we do not need to oppose parental imagery for God: "In expressing our relationship to the Lord as father or mother, it is not as if we are making God one or the other parent and pitting one against the other. Both fatherhood and motherhood give a particular insight into God's loving concern for human beings as individuals and as a group."[60]

The inclusion of female (and non-gender-related) language and imagery for God is not methodologically synonymous with the "add women and stir" prescription adopted as a corrective to male bias in educational research.[61] Far more than simply "adding" female imagery and language to existing male imagery and language, the recovery and restoration of the full range of biblical images for God *with* inclusive language for God can foster a new and transformative partnership among all persons in the church.

The Preface to the Brief Statement of Faith cites as a major function of confession of faith the need to draw on "a priceless heritage" to address present needs and so shape the future:

> Reformed confessions, in particular, when necessary even reform the tradition itself in the light of the Word of God. From the first, the Reformed churches have insisted that the renewal of the church must become visible in the transformation of human lives and societies. Hence "A Brief Statement of Faith" lifts up concerns that call most urgently for the church's attention in our time.[62]

Widening the margins of our language for both human beings and God can foster a creative and liberative renewal that enables the church to transcend the narrow limits of a male-exclusive rendering of human language and the world. Care must be taken to ensure that our language for God and our conceptualization of human experience and reality reflect both female and male reality, "otherwise one runs the double risk of denying God's image in the totality of creation, and failing to communicate the Good News at symbolic levels to all God's creation, women as well as men."[63]

The Brief Statement of Faith is a statement of our identity as a people who have been born anew and who are rooted in a commitment to theological and ecclesiological renewal: *Ecclesia reformata semper reformanda* (The church reformed is always in need of being reformed). The Brief Statement's verbal formulations can guide us on the journey, prompting us to adopt and use words and images that can promote justice in our linguistic transactions.[64] It can play a vital role in enhancing the transformation and renewal of the church. Widening the margins of language is indispensable in achieving a truly dynamic and life-bearing ecclesiology.

Notes

1. Jack Rogers, *Presbyterian Creeds: A Guide to the Book of Confessions* (Philadelphia: Westminster Press, 1985), pp. 25–26.
2. Ibid.
3. Casey Miller and Kate Swift, *The Handbook of Nonsexist*

Writing for Writers, Editors and Speakers, 2nd ed. (New York: Harper & Row, 1988), p. 1. Miller and Swift name such organizations and institutions as the American Psychological Association and the University of New Hampshire in their list of professional institutions and organizations that are seeking to eliminate linguistic sexism. Major public and private and local and national organizations, learned societies, professional and academic groups, and universities, colleges, and seminaries are mandating the adoption of guidelines to promote nonsexist language usage.

4. *The Power of Language Among the People of God and the Language About God: "Opening the Door": A Resource Document*, The United Presbyterian Church in the U.S.A., Task Force on Language About God, May 1975.

5. Gerda Lerner, *The Creation of Patriarchy* (New York: Oxford University Press, 1986), p. 239.

6. Dale Spender, *Man-Made Language* (Boston: Routledge & Kegan Paul, 1985), p. 52.

7. Ibid., pp. 52–53.

8. Ibid., pp. 53–54. See also Mary Daly, *Beyond God the Father: Toward a Philosophy of Women's Liberation*, 2nd ed. (Boston: Beacon Press, 1985).

9. Winnifred Tomm and Gordon Hamilton, eds., "Introduction," in *Gender Bias in Scholarship: The Pervasive Prejudice*, Calgary Institute for the Humanities series (Waterloo, Ontario, Canada: Wilfrid Laurier University Press, 1988), p. xv.

10. Gisele Thibault, "Women and Education: On Being Female in Male Places," in Tomm and Hamilton, eds., *Gender Bias in Scholarship*, p. 65.

11. Ibid.

12. Edwin Ardener, "Belief and the Problem of Women," in *Perceiving Women*, ed. Shirley Ardener (London: J. M. Dent & Sons, Malaby Press, 1975), pp. 1–28.

13. Estelle Dansereau, "Reassessing Interpretative Strategies in Literary Criticism," in Tomm and Hamilton, eds., *Gender Bias in Scholarship*, p. 49.

14. Marlene Mackie, "Sexism in Sociological Research," in Tomm and Hamilton, eds., *Gender Bias in Scholarship*, pp. 3–4;

and Pauline B. Bart, "Sexism and Social Science: From the Gilded Cage to the Iron Cage, or, The Perils of Pauline," *Journal of Marriage and the Family* 33 (1971), 734–735.

15. Thibault, "Women and Education: On Being Female in Male Places," p. 65.

16. Ibid., pp. 69, 89. The phrase "add women and stir" was coined by Charlotte Bunch, in "Visions and Revisions: Women and the Power to Change," *Women's Studies Newsletter* 7 (1979), 1–19.

17. Simon Podair, in *Phylon* (Fourth Quarter, 1956), quoted in Haig Bosmajian, "The Language of White Racism," *College English* 31 (December 1969), 263–272.

18. Cheris Kramarae, Muriel Schulz, and William M. O'Barr, "Toward an Understanding of Language and Power," in idem, eds., *Language and Power* (Beverly Hills, Calif.: Sage Publications, 1984), p. 9.

19. Haig A. Bosmajian, *The Language of Oppression* (Washington, D.C.: Public Affairs Press, 1974), p. 90.

20. Dennis E. Baron, *Grammar and Gender* (New Haven, Conn.: Yale University Press, 1986), p. 97.

21. Bosmajian, *The Language of Oppression*, p. 95.

22. Joan Huber, "And Some Are More Equal Than Others," *The American Sociologist* 2 (1976), 89.

23. Eric Marshall and Stuart Hample, *More Children's Letters to God* (New York: Simon & Schuster, Essandess Press, 1967). Cf. Nancy A. Hardesty, *Inclusive Language in the Church* (Atlanta: John Knox Press, 1987), p. 13.

24. See n. 4 above.

25. See "One in Christ—'An Inclusive-Language Lectionary,'" National Council of Churches (Office of Information, 475 Riverside Drive, Room 850, New York, NY 10115), n.d.; and see *An Inclusive-Language Lectionary*, 3 vols. (published for The Cooperative Publication Association by John Knox Press, The Pilgrim Press, and The Westminster Press): *Readings for Year A*, rev. ed., 1986; *Readings for Year B*, rev. ed., 1987; *Readings for Year C*, rev. ed., 1988.

26. The reader may consult such works on the subject as Nancy Hardesty's *Inclusive Language in the Church* and Brian Wren's

What Language Shall I Borrow? God-Talk in Worship: A Male Response to Feminist Theology (New York: Crossroad Publishing Co., 1989).

27. Rogers, *Presbyterian Creeds*, pp. 69–70. For a broader discussion of the range of issues, see also pp. 71–73.

28. Burton H. Throckmorton, Jr., "A Call for Inclusive Language in Scripture," in *Language and the Church: Articles and Designs for Workshops*, ed. Barbara A. Withers (New York: Division of Education and Ministry, National Council of the Churches of Christ in the U.S.A., 1984), p. 18. For other discussions of the subject of the significance of patriarchal cultural conditioning on the transmission and interpretation of biblical traditions, see Letty Russell, ed. (in cooperation with the Task Force on Sexism in the Bible, Division of Education and Ministry, National Council of Churches), *The Liberating Word: A Guide to Nonsexist Interpretation of the Bible* (Philadelphia: Westminster Press, 1976); Elisabeth Schüssler Fiorenza, *Bread Not Stone: The Challenge of Feminist Biblical Interpretation* (Boston: Beacon Press, 1986); Sallie McFague, *Models of God: Theology for an Ecological, Nuclear Age* (Philadelphia: Fortress Press, 1987).

29. Susan Brooks Thistlethwaite, "Inclusive Language Rooted in Biblical Authority," in Withers, ed., *Language and the Church*, p. 20.

30. Ibid. Cf. Madeline Boucher, "Scriptural Readings: God-Language and Nonsexist Translation," in Withers, ed., *Language and the Church*, p. 29. For a discussion of the ways in which females and males image God in the writings of Calvin and his contemporaries, see Jane Dempsey Douglass, *Women, Freedom, and Calvin* (Philadelphia: Westminster Press, 1985).

31. The literature on this subject is vast. Cf. John E. Stambaugh and David L. Balch, *The New Testament in Its Social Environment* (Philadelphia: Westminster Press, 1986); and Elisabeth Schüssler Fiorenza, *In Memory of Her: A Feminist Theological Reconstruction of Christian Origins* (New York: Crossroad Publishing Co., 1984).

32. Sallie McFague, *Metaphorical Theology: Models of God in Religious Language* (Philadelphia: Fortress Press, 1982), p. 17.

33. G. B. Caird, *The Language and Imagery of the Bible* (Philadelphia: Westminster Press, 1980), p. 174. John Macquarrie has aptly observed that metaphorical language regularly abounds in theological discourse. See his *God-Talk: An Examination of the Language and Logic of Theology* (New York: Harper & Row, 1967), pp. 97–100, 196–202.

34. McFague, *Metaphorical Theology*, p. 15.

35. Boucher, "Scriptural Readings: God-Language and Nonsexist Translation," p. 29.

36. James H. Cone, *My Soul Looks Back* (Nashville: Abingdon Press, 1982), p. 120.

37. David L. Shields, *Growing Beyond Prejudices: Overcoming Hierarchical Dualism* (Mystic, Conn.: Twenty-Third Publications, 1986), p. 30.

38. Elizabeth Carroll, "Can Male Domination Be Overcome?" *Women in a Men's Church*, ed. Virgil Elizondo and Norbert Greinacher, Concilium, 134 (4/1980) (New York: Seabury Press, 1980), p. 45.

39. Rosemary Radford Ruether, *Sexism and God-Talk* (Boston: Beacon Press, 1984), p. 66.

40. Mary Daly, *Beyond God the Father*, p. 19.

41. Ibid., p. 13.

42. David Buttrick, *Homiletic: Moves and Structures* (Philadelphia: Fortress Press, 1987), p. 8.

43. For a discussion of tensions in some of the images of God in biblical traditions see Phyllis Trible, *Texts of Terror: Literary-Feminist Readings of Biblical Narratives*, Overtures to Biblical Theology (Philadelphia: Fortress Press, 1984).

44. Ian T. Ramsey, "The Logical Character of Religious Language," in idem, ed., *Words About God: The Philosophy of Religion* (New York: Harper & Row, 1971), p. 209.

45. Charlie Westfall, "Images of God," *Grail* 3/2 (June 1987), 65.

46. Ruether, *Sexism and God-Talk*, p. 67.

47. Constance F. Parvey, "Language as Life-Bearing," *The Hymn* 34 (October 1983), 235.

48. David Willis, "What Belongs in a Future Ecumenical Creed? A Reformed Answer," in *An Ecumenical Confession of Faith?* ed.

Hans Küng and Jürgen Moltmann, Concilium, 118 (8/1978) (New York: Seabury Press, 1979), p. 64.

49. John H. Leith, *Creeds of the Churches: A Reader in Christian Doctrine from the Bible to the Present*, 3rd ed. (Atlanta: John Knox Press, 1982), p. 3.

50. Ronald Modras, "The Functions and Limitations of Credal Statements," in Küng and Moltmann, eds., *An Ecumenical Confession of Faith?* p. 39.

51. S. Mark Heim, "Gender and Creed: Confessing a Common Faith," *The Christian Century* (April 17, 1985), 379–381.

52. Savina J. Teubal, *Sarah the Priestess: The First Matriarch of Genesis* (Athens, Ohio: Ohio University Press, Swallow Press, 1984), p. xi.

53. John Van Seters, *Abraham in History and Tradition* (New Haven, Conn.: Yale University Press, 1975), p. 276.

54. Joseph Grassi, *God Makes Me Laugh: A New Approach to Luke*, Good News Study 17 (Wilmington, Del.: Michael Glazier, 1986), p. 16.

55. Ralph W. Klein, "Call, Covenant, and Community: The Story of Abraham and Sarah," *Currents in Theology and Mission* 15 (1988), 125.

56. Ibid., p. 121. Cf. Walter Brueggemann, "Impossibility and Epistemology in the Faith Tradition of Abraham and Sarah (Gen. 18:1–15)," *Zeitschrift für die Alttestamentliche Wissenschaft* 94/4 (1982), 615–634.

57. Edward J. Young, *The Book of Isaiah*, vol. 3: *Chapters 40–66*, New International Commentary on the Old Testament (Grand Rapids: Wm. B. Eerdmans Publishing Co., 1972), p. 284.

58. John L. McKenzie, *Second Isaiah*, Anchor Bible (Garden City, N.Y.: Doubleday & Co., 1968), p. 113. For a survey of the significance of female imagery for God in Isaiah 49:15, see Mayer I. Gruber, "The Motherhood of God in Second Isaiah," *Revue Biblique* 90 (1983), 351–359; John J. Schmitt, "The Motherhood of God and Zion as Mother," *Revue Biblique* 92 (1985), 557–569; Phyllis Trible, "Depatriarchalizing in Biblical Interpretation," *Journal of the American Academy of Religion* 41 (1973), 30–48.

59. Eduard Schweizer, *The Good News According to Luke* (Atlanta: John Knox Press, 1984), p. 247.

60. Bernard L. Marthaler, *The Creed* (Mystic, Conn.: Twenty-Third Publications, 1986), p. 34.

61. See above at notes 15 and 16.

62. Preface to "A Brief Statement of Faith: Presbyterian Church (U.S.A.)." A proposal to the 201st General Assembly (1989) from the Special Committee to Prepare a Brief Statement of the Reformed Faith; reprinted on pages 21–23.

63. Constance F. Parvey, ed., "Balancing the Theological Past: Male and Female Imagery," *Ordination of Women in Ecumenical Perspective: Workbook for the Church's Future*, World Council of Churches, Commission on Faith and Order; Faith and Order Paper 105 (Geneva: World Council of Churches, 1980), p. 45.

64. Marianne Sawicki, *Faith and Sexism: Guidelines for Religious Educators* (New York: Seabury Press, 1979), pp. 7–8.

God Overcomes Death with Life 7

Antoinette Clark Wire

The theme of the proposed Brief Statement of Faith seems to be that God is with us in life and in death, overcoming death with life. The statement begins, "In life and in death we belong to God," and it ends by confessing that "nothing in life or in death can separate us from the love of God in Christ Jesus our Lord." Between these two assertions of confidence we confess that God gave the world life and created all people equally in God's image to be one community. But we rebel against this God and threaten death to each other and to our planet, taking part in the sin of our world that cost Jesus his life. We confess that God raised him from the dead, vindicated his life, and delivers us with him from death to life. And we confess that God's Spirit renews life everywhere, baptizing us in living water and feeding us the bread of life so that we can embrace all life as loved by Christ and live holy and joyful lives together.

We who were given the task of writing this confession did not begin with this theme. We talked and wrote at length about the situation of our world that called for a confession today; but being a cross section of good Presbyterians, we could not agree. Sobered, we turned to the task of confessing God in hopes that our faith might be more shared than our analysis of the world. After much study of scripture and confessions, much discussion and writing, and talks with many people, we began to write. As the Brief Statement passed from one form to another, we found in it this thread of God's presence in life and death, overcoming death with life. Then we knew that there was a vision for our world that we did share, and we tried in our common confession of God to clarify it.

Looking back at previous confessions of the church, we can see clues of the situation in each case that provoked a confession of God. Early Christians confessed that "Jesus is Lord" when they recognized this man as God's own life among them. Later they confessed that Jesus was both divine and human to reclaim also the humanity of the one they worshiped. Reformation confessions appealed to God's sovereign Word over against oppressive church authority. The Barmen Declaration and more recent confessions in South Africa, Taiwan, and Korea claim faith in God alone, not in the state. The Confession of 1967 looks to God to reconcile black and white, male and female, nation and nation, while the Declaration of Faith calls up the long history of God's patience and pain as witness to God's sure faithfulness. We share in making all these confessions, and they give depth and definition to our lives. But what might it add in our time to confess God as one who knows death and yet gives life? Could this be our particular confession?

Let me propose this for consideration by pointing to three great crises we face today, any of which could destroy us. For life to win against death, in each case we need not only full and true data and the clearest eyes to see it, but we need an ultimate confidence that God wills life, and that, in spite of everything, life can come out of death. Only this can keep us working at such great and difficult tasks. Each of the three ways we confess God witnesses that God is particularly at work in one of these crises. So we know that through our labors and through means unknown to us, God will overcome death with life.

The planet is in crisis. The economic development which has come with industrialization and brought higher living standards and better health for many people has also threatened the natural environment in a number of ominous ways.[1] The visible threats of water and air pollution, soil erosion and shrinking natural habitats for plants and animals are the surface of unseen problems yet to come from such practices as using up fossil fuels and changing the gases in the atmosphere. Hopes for unlimited energy from nuclear power have been undermined by the Three Mile Island and Chernobyl accidents, waste disposal problems, and fear of proliferation of weapons-grade nuclear material. As more people on the planet join the profligate ways of Europe and America, problems can only intensify.

What does it matter in this kind of a crisis that we confess that God made all things good?[2] Can this magically keep the world safe from destruction and hold us back from following into extinction the other species whose habitats shrink and disappear? This confession may seem a weak branch to grab as our boat goes over the waterfall. But in fact there is great power in trusting God who created heaven and earth. Who else is trustworthy in a time when we find the best educated nations such as ours also the greatest perpetrators of pollution and exploitation of living things?

When we confess that God made all things good, we take the risk of choosing life over death. More than that, we recognize that God's creative work is not a product of our commitment, but that before we appeared and after we are gone the earth is constituted by a will for good. Our narrow glimpses into this universe teach us above all humility and respect, not only for the creature but also for the Creator, "from whom and in whom and to whom are all things" (Rom. 11:36, RSV alt.).

As we confess this Creator, we also confess that it is we who threaten death to the planet. Although every natural disaster is not of human making, it is we of the advanced industrial societies who are responsible for the particular death threat that now hangs over the earth. When we confess our sin, we are given freedom of resistance, which in this case is freedom to join in the long-term political struggle in each local place to restructure our life for the planet's recovery and continued health. In this way we human beings who have exploited the earth can reclaim our integral place within that created universe.

Second, the nations are also in crisis. This can be called the wealth-poverty crisis, or in our decade the debt crisis.[3] We prefer to focus on East-West conflicts where the contestants are more evenly matched in wealth and arms, but it is becoming clear that the real struggle is the so-called North-South struggle. Here both superpowers fear to lose their economic satellites and therefore give military "aid" to governing groups in these countries who then keep the exports coming.

The human cost of this long-standing economic exploitation with its "low intensity conflict" against local armed opposition is beyond measurement. The death count every year in each such country includes not only the armed on both sides, but also the civilians assassinated and "disappeared" and those, especially children and the elderly, who die of malnourishment and untreated diseases. The recent practice of making heavy loans to such governments to keep them afloat has led to the point that in 1988 the world's seventeen most-indebted countries paid the industrialized nations and world agencies over $31 billion more than they received in aid.[4] What this means is that the world's poorest nations are squeezed dry of money that should be going into basic health, education, subsistence agriculture, and human services. In one barrio in Peru the school-age children were recently weighed every month, and one third of the first-graders were losing weight.[5] This systemic problem cannot be solved by our visits and gifts, which only keep us informed. It requires immediate national and international plans for forgiveness of debts and a long-term political struggle to reshape the way nations are economically and politically related to each other.

Since the time of the Hebrew prophets, God's judgment has been spoken against those who "buy the poor for silver and the needy for a pair of sandals" (Amos 8:6). Exploitation is violence and generates opposition, which in turn generates yet greater violence by the exploiters to preserve their advantages.[6] Jesus' death cannot be understood without asking why he was executed, what he had done, and whom this threatened. He preached the good news of God's kingdom to the poor, healed the sick, ate with outcasts, exposed the evil practices of religious and political leaders, and demanded repentance. When we confess that Jesus was crucified, giving his life for the sins of the world, we are saying he suffered the ultimate violence of execution for what he did. It is this Jesus whom we confess God raised from the dead. God thus vindicated Jesus' life, and with him vindicated all those who suffer such injustice. By God's grace we are incorporated into that deliverance from death to life, as Paul adds, "provided we suffer with him in order that we may also be glorified with him" (Rom. 8:17). This means: provided that we enter into Christ's vindicated life through our confession and let his energy in us work with all God's suffering people for the deliverance of the nations.[7]

Finally, our communities are in crisis. I hesitate most to describe this crisis because we all know it from direct experience, and yet its form is not the same for everyone. In the last half-century the United States has changed from a country of towns and small cities oriented to farming and local industries, where most people were known to their neighbors and lived near family, to a country of large cities, large corporations, and individual people.[8] Some of these people are freer and richer than they used to be and have more chance to travel and change jobs. Yet the strain of the competitive workplace and the few close relationships with others have often impoverished life, leading to burnout, dysfunctional families, violence, depression, and escape-oriented recreation. Others have lost jobs, homes, spouses, or children and are easy prey for those trying to "make it" by manipulation of others, sexual exploitation, or selling drugs.[9] Institutions may assist without helping; and, in a society where everyone is supposed to be independent, many people have no place to turn, and some die. One is reminded of the line from an old confession of sin, "there is no health in us."

How can we in our alternately feeble and complicit churches have any impact on this conundrum too close for us to see? What does it mean to say that we trust God's Spirit, the giver and renewer of life? Again, the confession is no formula by which we can escape the work in every local place of envisioning and testing out new shapes for our common life. But without a Source of life, and without a community to witness to that Spirit, we cannot sustain this long-term work. Here we confess that God's Spirit binds us in the one body of Christ, integrating us by living water, nourishing us with the bread of life. Because of the sure belonging here where women and men share the ministry and struggle to claim all their lives for Christ, we are set free to live holy and joyful lives and to cooperate with all communities of good will in work for justice, freedom, and peace.

There is one particular danger in the confession of God's presence with us in life and death that must be faced and fought. It is possible in a time when people feel programmed into death-dealing systems to seek comfort and escape from responsibility by romanticizing death. This is symbolically depicted, for example, in a sequence in Richard Adams's novel *Watership Down.*[10] A group of migrating rabbits is tempted to settle into a well-fed warren where the local rabbits tell mystic and melancholy stories of suffering and death. The group almost loses one of its number to a trap before realizing that these rabbits are being fed so well in order to be eaten, and that they have resigned themselves to this fate.

The story of Jesus' death has sometimes functioned this way to pacify the oppressed with divine presence in suffering and promises of future life—to the advantage of others who live off their work. If the crises that face us are so immobilizing, so oppressive, that we withdraw into such a pseudo-Christian death-is-life mysticism, we directly counteract the whole work of God to overcome death with life. God has indeed given death its place in the natural order of life, but people have used this reality to threaten and control each other, imprisoning humanity in a spiral of violence. We believe that in Christ God broke through this deathly life with a new creation, a true community of equality and justice. When Jesus who lived this new order was crucified by and for human sin, God vindicated his life by raising him to eternal life as the "firstfruit" that assures the coming full harvest of life to follow. As far as we are from mastering the deep justice and wide mercy of God's will to life, we can name the death that we make for each other and our earth as its enemy, and we can fight it head on, knowing as we now do that God is overcoming death with life.

What, then, is the meaning of the statement that "in life and in death we belong to God"? Surely it incorporates God's presence with us and all people as we face the personal losses of natural death. But it means more. First, we are confessing that we trust our Creator, Christ, and Spirit to bring all life to full and mature fruit beyond our capacities of being and knowing. And second, we are confessing that we do not always trust in God. We are unfaithful confessors, withdrawing in fear to get relief, allowing the human-built structures of death to have their way. Because of our sin and its work of death, we must always begin again, and we can only begin again by reclaiming the assurance that "in life and in death we belong to God" and that "nothing in life or in death can separate us from the love of God in Christ Jesus our Lord." Our confidence is finally not even in life itself, to which we are not equal, but in God who has chosen to overcome death with life and who is faithful.

Notes

1. A comprehensive collection of illustrated articles and graphs introducing the multifaceted problems faced by our planet and its peoples appeared as a special issue of *Scientific American* 261/3 (1989) titled "Managing Planet Earth."

2. An important resource paper prepared by the Presbyterian Eco-Justice Task Force and issued by the Committee on Social Witness Policy, Presbyterian Church (U.S.A.), is titled *Keeping and Healing the Creation* (order through DMS, 100 Witherspoon Street, Louisville, KY 40202-1396). Other theological analyses of the ecological crisis have appeared in recent years: John B. Cobb, *Is It Too Late: A Theology of Ecology* (Beverly Hills, Calif.: Bruce, 1972); H. Paul Santmire, *The Travail of Nature* (Philadelphia: Fortress Press, 1985); Jürgen Moltmann, *God in Creation: A New Theology of Creation and the Spirit of God* (San Francisco: Harper & Row, 1985); Douglas John Hall, *Imaging God: Dominion as Stewardship* (Grand Rapids: Wm. B. Eerdmans Publishing Co., 1986); Thomas Berry, *The Dream of the Earth* (San Francisco: Sierra Club Books, 1988). See also the collection edited by Dieter T. Hessel, *For Creation's Sake: Preaching, Ecology, and Justice* (Philadelphia: Geneva Press, 1985). Biblical themes are linked to ecological in Walter Brueggemann's *The Land: Place as Gift, Promise, and Challenge in Biblical Faith* (Philadelphia: Fortress Press, 1977).

3. See *Minutes of the 201st General Assembly of the Presbyterian*

Church (U.S.A.), 1989, Part I: *Journal*, para. 40.163–.282: "The Third World Debt Dilemma: Searching for a Moral Response to Vulnerable People and Systems." This resource paper, prepared by the Committee on Social Witness Policy, reviews the debt crisis and provides biblical and theological background and implications for our church and government. The paper can be found in much-abbreviated form in *Church & Society*, July-August 1989, 35–40. For a brief and careful general description of debt conditions today see also Benjamin Cohen, *Developing Country Debt: A Middle Way*, Essays in International Finance, 173 (Princeton, N.J.: International Finance Section at Princeton University, May 1989). A general analysis and prognosis for North American Christians concerning world economic conditions is available in Walter L. Owensby's *Economics for Prophets: A Primer on Concepts, Realities, and Values in Our Economic System* (Grand Rapids: Wm. B. Eerdmans Publishing Co., 1988). See also J. Philip Wogaman, *Economics and Ethics: A Christian Inquiry* (Philadelphia: Fortress Press, 1986).

4. William D. Ruckelshaus refers to these statistics from the World Bank in his "Toward a Sustainable World," *Scientific American* 261/3 (1989), 174.

5. This and other evidence of hunger and panic among the Peruvian poor are described in an article by John McCoy in *Latinamerica Press* 20 (Dec. 29, 1988), 1–2.

6. A trilogy of theological studies reflecting on poverty from a Latin American Christian perspective is available through the World Council of Churches from Julio de Santa Ana, *Good News to the Poor: The Challenge of the Poor in the History of the Church* (1977); *Separation Without Hope* (1978); and *Towards a Church of the Poor* (1979) (Geneva: World Council of Churches).

7. Policy questions rising from biblical reflection on the economic crisis are reviewed in Richard Shaull's *Naming the Idols: Biblical Alternatives for United States' Policy* (Oak Park, Ill: Meyer Stone Books, 1988).

8. One prominent analysis of the problems of American individualism is Robert N. Bellah et al., *Habits of the Heart: Individualism and Commitment in American Life* (Berkeley: University of California Press, 1985).

9. In each area, studies are available through the church and secular presses. One example of the influence an analysis can have on people's perception of their condition can be seen in Anne Wilson Schaef's several recent studies including *When Society Becomes an Addict* (San Francisco: Harper & Row, 1987).

10. Richard Adams, *Watership Down* (Harmondsworth, Middlesex, England: Penguin Books, 1972), pp. 68–128.

Contributors

James D. Brown, M.Div., Pastor, St. Peter's by the Sea Presbyterian Church, Rancho Palos Verdes, California

Jane Dempsey Douglass, Ph.D., Hazel Thompson McCord Professor of Historical Theology, Princeton Theological Seminary, Princeton, New Jersey

George H. Kehm, Th.D., Professor of Theology, Pittsburgh Theological Seminary, Pittsburgh, Pennsylvania

John H. Leith, Ph.D., Pemberton Professor of Theology, Union Theology Seminary, Richmond, Virginia

Clarice J. Martin, Ph.D., Assistant Professor of New Testament, Princeton Theological Seminary, Princeton, New Jersey

William C. Placher, Ph.D., Professor of Philosophy and Religion, Wabash College, Crawfordsville, Indiana

Jack L. Stotts, Ph.D., President, Austin Presbyterian Theological Seminary, Austin, Texas

E. David Willis, Th.D., Charles Hodge Professor of Systematic Theology, Princeton Theological Seminary, Princeton, New Jersey

Antoinette Clark Wire, Ph.D., Professor of New Testament, San Francisco Theological Seminary, San Anselmo, California